# EVERYTHING YOU NEED TO KNOW ABOUT STARTING A COMPETITION BBQ TEAM (EXCEPT THE RECIPES)

# George Hensler

Published by Río Grande Books
925 Salamanca NW
Los Ranchos, NM 87107-5647
505-344-9382
www.nmsantos.com

Printed in the United States of America

Book Design: Paul Rhetts

Library of Congress Cataloging-in-Publication Data

Hensler, George W.
  Startin' the fire : everything you need to know about starting a competition BBQ team, (except the recipes) / George W. Hensler.
    p. cm.
  ISBN 978-1-890689-14-8 (pbk. : alk. paper)
  1. Barbecue cookery--United States. 2. Barbecue cookery--Competitions--United States. I. Title.
  TX840.B3H46 2010
  641.5'78407973--dc22
                        2009053858

Cover graphics by Patrick Carlson, www.bbqlogos.com.

# EVERYTHING YOU NEED TO KNOW ABOUT STARTING A COMPETITION BBQ TEAM (EXCEPT THE RECIPES)

# George Hensler

Río Grande Books
Los Ranchos, NM

# Table of Contents

Acknowledgements ................................................... 1

Foreword.............................................................. 3

Introduction ......................................................... 5

Chapter 1 Competitive cooking, is it a sport? .......................... 7
Chapter 2 So you've got an idea? ...................................... 8
Chapter 3 Making the commitment .................................. 11
Chapter 4 When a new guy not? ...................................... 13
Chapter 5 Cooker selection .......................................... 15
Chapter 6 New Holland Summerfest 2007 ........................... 18
Chapter 7 Team building ............................................. 24
Chapter 8 BBQ Folks/Good People/Good Friends ................... 26
Chapter 9 Selecting a team name .................................... 29
Chapter 10 Cooking skills ........................................... 31
Chapter 11 Transportation .......................................... 34
Chapter 12 Equipment selection ..................................... 36
Chapter 13 Contest ZZZZZ's, Necessary or overrated? ............... 38
Chapter 14 Practice contest ......................................... 45
Chapter 15 Chicken, chicken & more chicken, lonely world of a chicken man .... 47
Chapter 16 Intervention of sorts .................................... 50
Chapter 17 Site safety .............................................. 53
Chapter 18 The judges and organizers ............................... 56
Chapter 19 Your first contest ....................................... 57
Chapter 20 The Beltway BBQ Showdown 5/18-5/19 2007—Our First Contest .. 61
Chapter 21 Box building 101 ......................................... 63
Chapter 22 BBQ Gremlins; fact or fiction ........................... 69
Chapter 23 Food safety ............................................. 73
Chapter 24 Afterwards .............................................. 75
Chapter 25 Too much of a good thing? ............................... 77
Chapter 26 Shigging ................................................ 79
Chapter 27 A Playlist—Contest Tunes ............................... 83
Chapter 28 Final Thoughts .......................................... 87
Chapter 29 BBQ Terms .............................................. 88

Sources ............................................................ 97

About the Author .................................................. 99

# Acknowledgments

If you had asked me a year or two ago if I would ever write a book about starting a BBQ team I am sure I know what my response would have been. I really do not think the answer would have been yes. I am not even sure how it got to this point, but here it is. I cannot begin without thanking a few folks that I would consider as contributors to my BBQ exploits.

My Mom Marlene, whose cooking skills I still admire and guidance through life I could not have done without.

My wife, Jo Ann. Also my best friend, love of my life, sounding board, advisor, editor, agent, taste tester, assistant cook and all around good egg.

My three sons, Bill, Andy and Sam. My backbone, my buddies, the sparkle in me eye. These guys have eaten a ton of my BBQ, good and bad, laughed at my jokes, helped me make decisions, loaded the trailer, unloaded the truck, anything I asked, well, mostly anything. Sometimes they even lent a hand without complaining! Thanks guys.

My BBQ Mentor, Steve Farin. I met Steve in 2004 at the Bel Air BBQ Bash (Belair, Maryland). Since then he has shown me the ins and outs of competition BBQ as well as becoming a good friend. Thanks for everything Steve.

My 'who are those guys?' BBQ teammates from Street, Maryland, Al Smith, Bob Zengel, and Erich Schmitt. Great friends, good grub, cold beers, good times, and a lot of help. Thanks friends.

My editor and good friend, Jack Whelehan has been a great help to me over the years and an inspiration to me to follow my dream to write this book. Thanks.

Thanks to all the BBQ teams who provided logos to use in this book. And a special thanks to Patrick Carlson for creating the cover graphics.

# Foreword to Startin' the Fire
## by Dave DeWitt, aka "The Pope of Peppers"

I competed on the barbecue cookoff circuit one time, when I was part of the Beer :30 Cookoff Team with Dr. BBQ (Ray Lampe), Mike Stines, Ph.B., and the ultimate pig lover, Gwyneth Doland, who has the tattoo of a diagram of butcher's hog cuts on her lower back. We competed at the BarbeQLossal Pork Cookoff in Des Moines, and I drew the assignment of smoke-grilling pork tenderloins, which I had never done in my entire life. I have given cooking demonstrations to 600 people at the Scottsdale Culinary Festival without breaking a sweat, but competing professionally at a barbecue cookoff was very intimidating. My heart was pounding and my knees kinda shaky but I did my best and actually placed in the middle of the pack of 40-plus competitors. Not too bad for my first time.

So when George sent me his query for this book, I jumped on it like a pig on corn and knew we had to publish it because it is totally unique in the BBQ field. No recipes! No explaining that barbecue is different from grilling! Just all you need to know about forming a competition barbecue team. Being a certified Kansas City Barbeque Society (KCBS) cookoff judge, I relish BBQ professionalism, and George has it in spades—or grills.

# Introduction

You love BBQ, you enjoy cooking, when you prepare ribs for family and friends, they say you are the best. Now you want to start a competition BBQ team. You have watched the events on TV; perhaps you have attended a contest or two. Either way, you are giving it some thought. If the idea of hanging out for a day or two with some friends, all the while cooking up some good food sounds like something that would interest you, then I say go for it.

You could just back your vehicle into the garage, toss in everything you think you will need. Stop at the store to buy some meat and beer, and then drive down to the contest site. Oh, and on the way, pick up a couple of day laborers. This certainly would be the easy way, but would not be my suggestion. Although, I am sure it's been done many times in the past, with varying degrees of success. To enter a contest takes a commitment of time, effort

## COMPETITION BBQ TEAM
### NEW JERSEY

and money. In my humble opinion, unless you have some of each to burn, a little foresight is required.

Here you will find my suggestions for you to consider while planning for your entry into the world of competition BBQ. Please keep in mind; I just finished the second season with my team. I am by no means a BBQ expert, nor do I profess to be. I do consider my self a decent organizer and planner. Good preparation and proper planning can go a long way in both your enjoyment and the overall outcome of a competition. While planning and preparation alone will not help you cook good BBQ, it will make you feel a lot better about your effort when the day is done, no matter where you finish.

This book will detail and expound on the process of organizing a competition BBQ team, from your initial idea, to cooking in your first full contest. We will cover preliminary considerations, planning, equipping, set-up, and running your own team. I will discuss what I feel is necessary to get your team into its first season of competition. Included will be discussions on box building, site preparation and safety, equipment choice and organization, the judging process and much more. My experience is with the KCBS series, but much of the information can be used elsewhere as well, as it is not specific to KCBS.

What will not be covered here is cooking techniques, methods, seasonings, rubs, recipes etc. as that is beyond the scope of this book. I will leave these discussions to those with more BBQ cooking experience than I. (Which will include most of the other cooks on the current circuit.) I will, however, offer my opinion on how to improve your skills once you have made the commitment start a team.

Competition BBQ cooking can be great fun. It is a chance to get out and spend some time with friends and family. You will meet many good folks along the way. The main objective is to do well in a contest. To me, if you are not enjoying the experience, you might as well just stay home. Take along some good food to prepare for your team and have fun, that's what it's all about.

Enjoy yourself!

# Chapter 1

**Competitive cooking, is it a sport?**

I finally found a competitive sport that I like. I tried my hand at golf, but never had much interest. Besides, it takes too long to play a round these days, what with all of the slow playing women on the course (just kidding girls.) My vertical leap is not quite good enough for the NBA, close, not off by much, and I got that age thing working against me. Bull riding is out. World Series of Poker costs too much just to buy in and I have trouble seeing the cards with sunglasses on. Nope, BBQ looks like a winner. Good friends, cold beer, beef, chicken, pork, and sauce. (All the major food groups covered.) Now there is a sport you can really sink your teeth into. Any sport where one of the first steps is to rub your meat is OK in my book. Vegetarians need not apply.

I know, I know, there are some who will say, competitive cooking, that's not a sport. I used to get into these arguments with guys at work all the time. These same guys would say NASCAR, that's just driving in a circle, no sport there. Then they would go home and watch golf, poker, billiards or competitive hot dog eating on ESPN. Correct me if I am wrong, but if competitive eating is shown on the nation's premier sports channel, then it must be a sport. And if the eating is a sport, why can't the cooking of those hot dogs or in this case BBQ be a sport? My dog-eared copy of Merriam-Webster's says, sport: noun- /'sport/a source of diversion: recreation, physical activity engaged in for pleasure.

'Nuff said, I think we have those requirements covered here.

It's probably a good thing too, that BBQ is my sport. You have heard how "they" say he has the frame of a halfback, or, he has the hands of a quarterback, or, he has a body built for wrestling. I never quite heard anything of this sort when I was growing up. I will spare the gory details of the comments that were, and continue to be, hurled my way. One thing for certain, I have a body built for BBQ, there is not much dispute to this statement. A hot greasy smoker, surrounded by friends and family, some good tunes, a couple of stains on my shirt, cold beer in my hand, all shrouded in a sweet smelling blue smoke, that's what I am talking about! That's what I call livin'. It really don't get no better than this.

# Chapter 2

**So, you've got an idea?**

The initial thought and pondering has occurred and you still think you are interested. It is time for a little legwork and research. You already have the basics down on how to cook some que. If you are not familiar with how to cook all of the different meats, not to worry, as we will also discuss this later in the book.

My first suggestion would be to talk to someone that cooks on a team. Attend a contest or two and see what it's all about. While you are walking around the contest site, talk to the cooks and ask questions. Most are more than willing to discuss BBQ at the drop of a hat. One word of advice here would be to not interrupt if they are involved with prep work or contest turn-ins. This is a busy time and folks are not in the mood to talk during busy times. Fridays, any time, and Saturdays before 11:00am, after 2:00pm are usually the best times to visit with the cooks.

Plan to visit on both Friday and Saturday if you can. While a BBQ contest is not a fan friendly spectator sport, there is a lot to see if you know what to look for. On Friday, the teams will be trimming and prepping their meats getting them ready for the cookers. Late Friday evening, many will be lighting their smokers and loading in the big meats, (briskets & butts), some of these take 10-12 hours to cook. Saturday mornings they will be finishing their meats and building the turn-in boxes. Many teams operate behind curtains and in motor homes for obvious reasons, but there are plenty that have their prep tables well within the view of the casual observer. Wander around; most competitors are very friendly folk. Many will strike up a conversation with you, most enjoy talking BBQ and if you show an interest, they will usually answer questions. Just be discrete and if it appears the person doesn't want an audience, just move on.

In some areas, depending on the local Health Department regulations, teams will offer samples after all of the turn-ins are complete. If this happens, it is a great way to sample some competition quality grub. Just remember, it's a sample, not lunch, so save some for the next guy. We have had folks come into our site and ask for a plate and foil to wrap a "to go" package. I find this just a tad pushy, so use discretion and common sense.

If possible, attend the awards ceremony, which is usually held on Saturday afternoon. Here you will see the teams and competitors getting the recognition from the judges with trophies, ribbons, and maybe some cash. You will also observe the accolades given to the other teams by their fellow competitors. Most times there is a great display of good sportsmanship.

Each team is anxious to hear their name called so they can take the coveted "walk" to the stage. This is what they all entered for.

Grab a note pad and make a plan. Commit your thoughts and ideas for your team to paper. Establish a time line of how you want to proceed. Where will the funding come from? What equipment is needed? Who will participate? In short, create a sort of a BBQ business plan to assist with the organization, just be sure to use a pencil with a big eraser, as there will be plenty of changes.

Read any thing you can get your hands on about BBQ. Visit BBQ forums and read the threads. Most of the better forums have tremendous archives and search capabilities, look around, then read some more. The BBQ Forum, www.rbjb.com/rbjb/rbjbboard, is a great resource for all information about BBQ. Also, be sure to visit The BBQ Brethren Forum, www.bbq-brethren.com. Visit web sites of existing teams. Many post pictures of their products and the contests they have cooked. Many good books about competitive BBQ cooking are out there as well. My recommendation here would be DR. BBQ's Big Time Barbecue Cookbook. This book is very helpful with insight, technique, and recipes from a proven BBQ champion. The good Doctor has several books on the market, all of which are permanent additions to my personal collection.

While doing your research it is a good idea to start a notebook. A binder, some dividers and a three-hole punch are cheap enough, you might even have them around the house somewhere not in use. When you come across an item that looks to be informative and or helpful, print it out and file it in your book. Share the information with your teammates if they are

interested. With today's technology, most items can be sent via e-mail. That is, providing your teammates know how to use the Internet. Organize your notes anyway you see fit; my only suggestion is have it done in such a way that when you are looking for a paper on a topic, you can find it.

There are also many local and regional BBQ associations, so search around and become a member. It's a great way to meet folks with similar interests. Many of these local groups will sponsor BBQ shows from time to time. Attend a show, look at the cookers, visit with supply/equipment vendors, many shows will have actual cooking demonstrations ongoing, again, a good information source. Local BBQ societies are also a great place to find a BBQ mentor and or a team to assist.

Once you have talked a few folks into following this pipe dream of yours about starting a BBQ team, visited a few contests, scratched a few ideas down on paper and taken a second mortgage on the family house, you are ready to move on to Chapter 3.

# Chapter 3

## Making the Commitment

You have been to a few contests and done some reading on the subject. You have spoken to a few friends and it looks like there is some interest. Are you ready to commit? So far, other than the cost of a few things that you have purchased, you have no real money invested. Is it time to start writing checks? Not just yet, you still have a little more groundwork to do.

Try and get involved. Ask around at the contests that you have attended, check with a local BBQ society or make a post on a BBQ forum, look for a team with the "help wanted" sign out. Volunteer to help. Wash dishes, scrub grill gates, clean the cooker, run boxes, bag trash, anything that needs doing to get to a contest or two. It's the only way to get the real flavor of what goes on. Many folks on the BBQ circuit need help from time to time and most are willing to help someone get their feet wet, show you the ropes so to speak.

If you are lucky enough to get on with a team in a contest, don't show up empty-handed. You are going to be spending many hours there, bring along some drinks and something for everyone to nibble on. You wouldn't show up to your friend's house empty-handed would you?...well...let's just say, these guys are offering to let you hang around in hopes of learning something, so it would be a good idea to bring some refreshments for both you and them.

While on site, volunteer to do anything. Naturally, grate cleaning and trash removal are some of the less popular jobs. Nobody likes to do them, so jump in and get them done. Anticipate, if the trash bag is full, tie it off, haul it to the dumpster and install another bag. The grates need scrubbing, get out a brush. Show some initiative, some hustle, some interest. Don't just sit around, drinking their beer, eating their food and asking stupid questions (like I did).

Don't be nosy. The team will be involved in steps and processes that they are using in competition. Use discretion, watch and help when it appears you are welcome. Don't be afraid to ask if you should step away and let them alone for certain steps. They will let you know what to do and what they don't mind you observing. Don't be too pushy and ask too may questions. What I am saying here is, be discrete. You do not want to wear out your welcome.

Be appreciative that someone is willing to share the experience with you. This may sound like a simple concept; however, it is often overlooked. Above all, don't blab about what you have seen. You would be surprised how many times I was approached at contests where I was a dishwasher and asked specific questions about what was going on at the site where I was helping. My advice, dummy up, like Sgt. Schultz on *Hogan's Heroes*......I know *nothing*!

# Chapter 4

### When a new guy not?

As you may or may not know, our team is fairly new to competition BBQ cooking. In 2008, we competed in seven events and have six on the schedule for 2009. As I sit around and ponder, awaiting the start of the season, the question comes to my mind, when do you lose the title of newbie, new guy, and or rookie? Not that there is anything wrong with the monikers, I sort of like them.

I wonder, when does a team move forward and become just another member of the circuit. Is it after your first competition, your fifth, your first season, the first call, or your first Grand Championship? Or, is it option Z, there is there no real bar or plateau to reach, it just sort of goes away like rising smoke, the more experience you accumulate and the way you look at yourselves, the way you feel. Your own comfort level.

Our team is a group of four guys and my wife; we have been friends for many years before we were teammates. We came together and formed a team, entered some contests, and even got a few calls. We had a lot of fun and met many great new friends. The group is looking forward to the upcoming season, not only for the companionship, but also for the learning experience that comes with every event we attend. We enjoyed the forming of our team and the learning that goes along with the process. We look forward to improving our skills and our efficiency, and to the learning that occurs each time we fire up our cooker.

In our minds, we are still rookies with a lot to learn. The new season comes with much anticipation. Each time we discuss Que among ourselves or with others on the circuit, we are striving to learn, to improve, and to make our product better. We take what we have already learned, combine it with our new information, and move forward in hopes of doing better our next time out.

Do we mind being considered newbies? Heck no. We really enjoy the anonymity that comes with being a new team. We enjoy coming in where we are not known and making new friends. Staying under the radar, being unknown. Of course it goes without saying, once you get to know our gang, you'll want to stay as far away from us as possible! Just kidding, we hope that some day folks may say to themselves, "who ARE those guys?" and that would be a good thing!

What about if you were ever fortunate enough to get a first time invitation to The Jack or a similar prestigious contest, wouldn't you, in effect, again, be a newbie? Would you be nervous, ask many questions, try to learn everything you could before you arrived? Sounds like a newbie to me.

I am sure we will feel more comfortable attending the contests that we have been to in the past, as would anyone going back where you have already been. It's sort of like going to a friend's house that you have visited once before, you feel somewhat at ease.

However, one event this year will be a new experience for our team, again, we are the newbies. I equate this experience to back when you were a teenager, for those of you that can remember back that far, I know it is a little foggy for me. Remember going to visit the home of a girl you were dating for the first time. You knew she lived in a *house*, you knew what a *house* was, you've even been in a *house* before, but you were very apprehensive, even just knocking on the door, nervous would be an understatement.

The more that I burn what little brain cells that I have left on this topic, the more that I think the answer to my question is option Z. I think you will realize it when it happens. When you stop telling folks that ask, "This is our third year," before you tell them anything else. When you show up and know what to do without asking questions. But most of all, what I consider the most important part of the entire process, is when you start to answer questions for others, instead of always asking them. Paying it forward, so to speak. Passing what you have learned, through listening and watching others, along with your own experience, onto others with the same desire to learn that you have, and had, when you first decided to enter into this crazy sport/addiction/hobby/lifestyle called BBQ.

When you find yourselves answering more questions than asking, that's when I think you are no longer a newbie. You have arrived. As for the "who are those guys?" gang, we are still newbies with a lot to learn. We look forward to asking many questions and searching for the answers. We also hope, that as time goes on, we will be able to provide reasonable answers to a few questions asked by others, to help the next guy get involved or improve. Just as many have done for us.

Moving forward into the coming season are we still newbies? I think so. We will wear the name proudly. Maybe I wouldn't call us rookies, but newbies for sure. Are we somewhat confident and nervous at the same time? Yes. Are we apprehensive? Oh yeah, a lot…. what if her father answers the door!

# Chapter 5

## Cooker Selection

I found as I poked around for info that there are as many opinions about cookers and fuels as there are cooks. Many are very passionate about the topic to the point of accusing others of being illegal, or at the very least, "not really BBQing."

If you do not already have a cooker that you are using, you may need to spend some time researching and testing various cookers for competition use. As I previously stated, there are many different types of smokers available in today's marketplace. You also have the option of making your own. Some folks are very handy and can make just about anything they put their mind to. I am not one of those fellows. I have trouble changing a light bulb without a safety net.

There are the horizontal and or offset style cookers. At a cook-off you will see many variations of these units. Some are known as stick burners, which use mainly wood for fuel. It is just my opinion, but it always seems to me that some of the wood burning guys are always fooling with their cookers to maintain a steady temperature. Looks like a lot of work to me, but it appears that those fellows are enjoying playing with the fire.

Upright box type smokers are very popular among some of the teams. There are several very popular brands on the market. They can be fueled by either wood or charcoal. Some have water pans used to defuse or deflect the heat emitting from the firebox.

Pellet burners or pellet poopers as they are known, use wood pellets of various flavors added to the firebox with an electric auger type setup. The pellets are similar to those burned in home pellet stoves. These cookers usually require a power source to be able to operate.

You also have folks who use ceramic cookers like the Big Green Egg. These cookers look very interesting to me. I have never cooked on one, but I have it on my list of things to do. Bullet style smokers like the Weber Smokey Mountain are also popular on the contest trail. They are inexpensive to purchase new when compared to some of the previous mentioned styles. Grate space is sometimes a consideration with the Smokey Mountain as well as the Big Green Egg.

In addition to choosing a cooker and deciding on what fuel to use, you must also determine if you will plan to employ any of the available cooker options. As you examine the market, you will find there are numerous systems for controlling your heat source and or assisting with your overall cook.

Be sure to research any option thoroughly before you buy. Make sure that the equipment is legal in the series that you plan to compete in. Also, it is a good idea if the unit or option that you are considering requires electric, that you be sure that you will be able to provide the needed power to operate either by generator by some type of a conversion system. Most contests supply electric. As with any temporary electric setup, sometimes there are power problems. You want to be sure to have a backup power source if needed. Be sure to check that any option you are considering is compatible with your cooker. Check with the manufacturer or supplier to be sure that it is available.

Ease of transportation is also a factor you should needed to take into account, as well as space to be able to hold all of the meat you would need to cook for a BBQ contest. The average team cooks two briskets, two butts, 4 slabs of ribs and at least 12 pieces of chicken.

Many suppliers and or manufacturers will offer you to let you "test drive" their equipment. This is a very good idea if you are not familiar with exactly how a cooker performs. You can take the unit home and actually cook on it to determine if it is something that you would consider purchasing. If they do not have a unit for you to try, ask for a list of a few satisfied customers and for permission to contact them. I would also again suggest searching the various BBQ forums and bulletin boards. Make a post or check the archives to see what others are saying about the cooker you are considering. Some of the larger manufacturers have their own web sites that also contain posts and comments from other users.

Do not be afraid to use a couple of different types of cookers in combination during a contest. Most important is knowing how the unit you are using performs, and how to maintain an even temperature throughout the cook.

Many teams will also bring some type of grill along. These can be handy for preparing camp chow. Some teams will use a grill to cook their chicken. Many employ the grill for setting sauces and finishing other meats. If you have room, they are a welcomed addition to the regular equipment list.

I have observed many spirited discussions during my time spent on BBQ forums as to the pros and cons of these and many other types of cookers and options. My personal thought is no matter what cooker you choose; the important thing is to learn the unit and how it cooks, with consideration given to what you as a cook want to do with the unit.

If you determine that you have to purchase a cooker, I would suggest trying to buy one on the secondary market, as in used, strictly to help lower the startup costs. Many BBQ forums have sections to buy and sell used equipment.

Some cooks would be more satisfied with buying a new unit. If you are thinking of a new unit, do not wait to the last minute to place your order. As the BBQ season approaches, many of the cooker builders develop long wait times. Some have a wait year round. The best advice here is to communicate with the maker of the cooker you are interested in and inquire how long the wait is. Bottom line, order early if possible.

# Chapter 6

## New Holland Summer Fest August 2007

The smoke had barely settled from the contest at Bel Air and it was time to prep for New Holland. In addition to the regular KCBS categories, there would be two optional cooks, chefs' choice and sausage. These categories would not count toward the KCBS section of the contest. Jo, my wife had volunteered to cook the chefs' choice and the team would do the sausage entry. We only had to gather up the meats, beer and garnish then we were all set. Al met me at my house around 9:00am on Friday then we set out for the drive up to New Holland, PA. We used Map Quest and took the back way through the scenic farm country of York and Lancaster Counties. The area is rich with beautiful farms, many owned and operated by Amish families, so this is always a very enjoyable ride.

We arrived at the Lions Park in New Holland around 11:00 and were quickly directed to our site, we were not the last to arrive. Over half of the teams were already in place. It is easy to see why this contest is a favorite for the teams on the BBQ circuit. It is a beautiful location and the organizers really take care of the contestants. Plenty of ice, free breakfast, reliable electric hook ups, well organized, clean rest rooms, and good music. The crowds here are also very friendly; it's just a good all-round deal.

The cooks' meeting was set for 6:00pm; Bobby and I set off to represent our team. This meeting is where the contest organizers and KCBS representatives answer questions, explain the rules, and give the cooks any last minute information. The official clock used for the turn in times is usually present at the meeting and the teams can use it to set their own clocks in hopes of not being late with an entry, at least due to a time misunderstanding.

The last part of the meeting is where the turn-in boxes are passed out to the teams to submit their entries the next day. The team names were being called in the order that they registered for the contest. This would make our team towards the very end of the 72-team field, as we were one of the last in the door due to coming in off the waiting list. As each team name was called, they went forward to pick up their boxes, then left the room for their respective sites.

This is when it hit me. Intimidated would be putting it lightly. Some of these teams I had seen on the Food Network, many I had read about during my many years of surfing BBQ web sites and other BBQ publications, many were winners of multiple Grand Championships, and some guys had their own line of spices and BBQ rubs. And there we were, 'who are those guys?'

I wonder if it's too late to get our entry fee back and break for the door. Just kidding, but I gotta tell you, I *was* intimidated, confident, a little, but definitely intimidated. I am glad that was over, gimme a beer.

At the appropriate time, the big meats went into the smoke and we took off for some meet and greet. We were getting the hang of this. We walked, talked and had a generally good time looking at cookers and talking BBQ with the other competitors. We even saw one team that was in the process of removing all the skin from their chicken thighs, scraping the fat from the underneath with a surgical knife, then replacing the skin. That looked like a lot of work, and I thought we spent a lot of time with *our* chicken. As we drifted past the stage, which was set with all of the trophies in preparation for the next day's awards, Al pointed at third place chicken trophy and said, "That's ours." I think my reply was something along the lines of, "yeah right," but chances are, it was a little more colorful than that!

The night was uneventful and daybreak found me getting the ribs into the smoke. A quick check on our butts and briskets found everything where I wanted it to be, temperature wise. The guys at Smoken Dudes do a nice breakfast for the teams on Saturday morning and this year was no different. Everyone was feeling good as we sat around the site after eating, for a little down time, the calm before the storm you could say. The morning just had that feeling, it was going to be a hot one and there was not one thing we could do about it. We did bring along a couple of box fans to put into strategic locations around the site to move a little air, but hot air moving is almost as hot as hot air sitting still, or something like that, anyway, it was warm and soon to get hot.

The chicken was in the smoker, in what I thought was plenty of time, but I could not get it to temperature. It was hanging around at about 140-150 and we did not have time to waste. I will have to admit, I got into a bit of a tizzy. The chicken was standing still and the clock was ticking. We had not started to apply sauce and finish the yard bird off, as we could not get it cooked. We had an indirect fire going in the Weber Kettle that we use to set our sauces. I called for the chicken to be moved to the Weber on the direct side in an attempt to get some heat and increase the internal temp.

One thing you do not want is undercooked chicken. The fire in the kettle was not very hot so this was not doing much, but it seemed like at least we were doing something. Al was on the grill and kept telling me not to worry as I drifted further and further into panic mode. The chicken came to temp and the sauce was set. I built the box without too much panic and Bobby took off for the judges, we made it with time to spare. I took a piece of chicken to taste from the pan that didn't make it into the box and it was lousy, I took two bites and gave it a pitch, well, we were in the tank already I thought. I hoped that things would get better, it sure was getting hot.

Chicken and sausage were in, and it was just past 12:00 noon, only 4 more categories to go, I felt like it was late afternoon and we should be cleaning up. Did I mention that it was a little warm? Well it was down right hot! How hot was it? It was hotter than a .......well you get the picture. Miserably hot. We slugged through the remaining turn-ins for the KCBS meats. Jo was doing the chefs choice and had chosen a crab dish that we served in a crab shell, surrounded with a dozen extra large BBQ shrimp. I helped her get the dish in the box and ran it to the scoring table as the heat had gotten the best of our runner Bobby. He was in a chair, in the shade, taking in needed fluids, he looked rough. One down.

After Jo's dish was in, it was past 2:00, we started to break down the site. It seemed like it was getting hotter by the minute. Someone asked me where something went in the trailer and my answer was anywhere that it fits, just throw it in. I think my real answer here was "it goes up your ***," but I am trying to keep this a family show. We tried to leave two canopies up until last so that we would have a little reprieve from the sun, but eventually, they were broken down and tossed in.

We grabbed our folding chairs and moved up to the picnic grove near the stage where there were a few shade trees. It was none too soon for me as I was just starting to get cold chills and I knew that was not good. We got under the trees and I located some ice, which I passed around to anyone who wanted it. I used the ice as a cooling pack and continued to take in water as I began to develop a pounding headache. The good news was that the chills had subsided; the bad news was I began to experience severe cramps or charley horses in my legs. Some of them so bad I had to get up and walk around. Jo, who is a nurse, said it was from the lack of electrolytes. Another note to self, pack some Gatorade or some other sport drink in the cooler for summer contests. Everyone was feeling the effects from the heat as we sat and waited for the awards to begin, there was not much idle chitchat.

Did I mention the word chafing, an unpleasant word that's for sure. Webster defines the word chafing as heat, wear, or soreness caused by rubbing. That pretty much nails it. Particularly unpleasant for me this weekend. The air was very hot, couple that with the radiant heat coming off the grill and cooker and we are talking scorching hot here. The kind of heat that causes you to sweat just standing still. Unfortunately for me, I was not just standing still, I was soaked and I was walking about.

CAUTION: THE REMAINING SENTENCES IN THIS PARA-GRAPH MAY NOT BE FOR THE MEEK OR THE FAINT AT HEART. PLEASE SKIP TO THE NEXT SECTION IF YOU HAVE A WEAK STOMACH OR CANNOT STAND HORRID IMAGES. PLEASE BE ADVISED, YOU HAVE BEEN WARNED. READ ON AT YOUR OWN RISK.

The combination of sweat soaked underwear and continual walking around results in an unwanted uncomfortable condition called chafing. This is a result of the rubbing of wet under garments across wet skin in the crotchel area over and over and over. I am not sure that crotchel is a word as it does not show up in my latest copy of Webster's, but I think that it should be and it certainly applies here. This condition can be very annoying if the afflicted is a slightly overweight, big headed, middle-aged, BBQ wannabe. A long time tighty-whitey man, well, you get the point. I was going to at-tach an image here but decided against it, I think you get the visual without it, you can thank me later. Another note to self, include a few changes of underwear and some Gold Bond ointment or powder into the must bring list, especially if the temperature is predicted to be over 95 in the shade. In short, try to avoid chafing in the crotchel area at all costs.

The contest folks at New Holland had decided to call to the stage the top 15 places for the KCBS meats which I thought was a great idea considering the size of the field. Sausage was first; we did not get a call. Then came the chefs' choice, I really thought ours had a chance, no call. Don't sweat it, I told myself, this was only our third contest and look who was here, we were lucky to even get in, as this contest has a waiting list every year. They would call places 15-11 as a group, then begin the single call out for 10th-1st.

Chicken was next, maybe we could grab one of the 15-11th places, wait a minute, the chicken I ate tasted like seagull, no way were we getting a call in chicken. The third place chicken winner is, Al looked over at me, we waited, "who are those guys?".... What heat? I sprang from my chair as if I had been shot from a gun, this cannot be happening. My formally cramped up legs gave me a temporary pass as I just about jogged up to receive our award. On the way up and back other cooks would offer handshakes and or congratulations, I could not believe it. Upon returning to our spot, I passed the trophy around for the guys to see, handshakes and congrats were a plenty. We would have been satisfied to go home right there, but fortunately for us, we decided to hang around. Third place chicken at New Holland now that was all right!

The next category was ribs, I thought ours looked and tasted good. The judges agreed, we got a call for 8th place pork ribs. As I walked to the stage to except the ribbon for our ribs, the announcer said, "I have a feeling by the end of today we're gonna know who these guys are!" Pretty cool.

The next call was for pork, certainly not our strong suit. Again, as before, I was not happy with our pork entry. I thought it looked and tasted like pot roast, not good. At least I remembered to include the sauce, but it did not help, at least in my opinion. We listened intently for our name for each place but it was not to be, no call in the pork category. I, for one, wasn't surprised. During the pork awards, my legs began to cramp again, so much that I had to leave my seat and go stand in the back of the crowd. Jo left her seat and came back to stand with me, I guess in case I was to keel over.

Brisket was next and I will tell you with two calls under our belt, I was really feeing good, with the exception of my severe headache, cramping legs, and aforementioned friction issue. Without another call all day, we would have been very satisfied. I still paid attention from my perch all the way in the back of the crowd, I wasn't hurting that bad. Second place brisket goes to….."Who are those guys?"...wow….three calls including a second in brisket, we might have a chance.

After the brisket walk I returned to my seat, wouldn't you know it, the cramps were gone again. I have to tell you, my old memory is a little foggy from this point forward. I think it was a combination of shock, disbelief, heat and too much beer the day before but my recollection of the overall awards is sketchy at best. I was sitting next to Al and I whispered over, we have a real chance here, that's about all I remember. The teams were called and they were getting closer and closer to the top spots. Our name not mentioned yet, was the pork that bad? Was it disqualified? My head was spinning, and when a head the size of mine gets to spinnin, you had better watch out.

The announcer was down to third overall when he called out our name, I could not believe it, third at New Holland. I motioned to the team to come with me as they had always been reluctant in the past to walk up to the stage. They all stood and we walked together to get the trophy. It was a great feeling. We had our picture taken and several other teams called out to us, what a ride. We returned to our seats and attempted to sit but there was way too much excitement for all of that.

A check of the scoring sheet showed our total score as 651.4286, the winner was 654.2854; man, we were close. Our pork finished 39th overall; respectable, but oh what if.

We were 24th in sausage and 15th in chef's choice. A lot later we found out that most of the top scores in the chef's choice category were desserts. This made too much sense. The chef's choice was the last to go in, the judges had been sampling BBQ foods for two hours, why wouldn't they want something sweet, another lesson learned.

I burned up the battery on my cell phone during the drive home. I called my sons, my mother, my friends, anyone I could think of to tell the story of our good fortune. At one point I dialed a wrong number and I told that guy how we did, he wasn't impressed and threatened to turn me in for an annoying phone call, oh well, everyone else liked the story. I even think I called Jo who was driving just ahead of me to ask her if this was all a dream, it wasn't.

We had come into New Holland as a new team and a last minute entry and finished third overall out of 72 teams. I really could not believe it. I know we had a great deal of luck with us, but I also think we were on the right track, or at the very least, we were close to the track. It seemed that some judges liked our product; at least they had so far. Time would tell.

# Chapter 7

## Team Building

Chris Capell from Dizzy Pig BBQ Company gave me some great advice as I spoke with him in New Holland, 2006 about starting my own team. "Get a group of folks that share your vision and you won't go wrong," he said. As simple as this concept seems, it is not always achievable. In my case, however, I think it was. I knew I had a good group of guys, as all were my friends for many years. But in addition to the friendships, everyone was excited about the idea in general. Everyone was looking forward to the upcoming season to see what we could learn and to see what this competition cooking was all about. In short, I think I had found four friends that shared my vision. I considered myself very fortunate.

You could go at it alone. There are several folks on the circuit who compete solo, maybe using someone from time to time to help with dishes and box running. This is a personal decision you will have to make. My opinion is the entire experience is much more enjoyable, not to mention easier, when you have a few good people around. It can also help to offset some of the operational expenses.

To help defray the costs and to assist with the labor involved, I would suggest trying to find a few suckers….I mean friends, to come along for the ride. As stated previously, try to find a few folks that share your interest and vision. It also does not hurt if they are interested in cooking. Although this is not a requirement, it is very helpful. You could try to use family members. There are many very successful husband and wife teams around. For my wife and me, this arrangement would never work. We would be in divorce court for sure or one of us would be in jail.

Team organization and operation is varied. You can decide early on or just let it evolve on its own. My advice would be to square it away before you get out of the gate, you can always make changes or adjustments as needed.

The first thing you need to do is name yourself the Chief. You can call it the boss of the sauce, head chef, dictator, pit master, chief cook, postmaster general, grand poobah, president, CEO, or just plain King. Someone has to be in charge, call the shots, and make the decisions. Since it was your idea, and you have all of the time invested so far, it looks like you are the one. You could as one of your first official duties name someone else to the position. I would advise against that one. You had better declare yourself in charge and get it out in the open right now, to avoid any confusion or misunderstanding down the road. Every team needs someone to be the boss, to take credit when things go right, and to assign blame when they go wrong, just like at work. The only exception to this declaration is when the wife is on site; we all know who's the boss then, don't we?

Divide the responsibilities. If you are lucky enough to have a few team members, ask each to be responsible for a task. Assign a member to plan and shop for the team food and drink; another can get the contest meats and the ice, and so on. This helps reduce the work and stress before a contest.

I think it's also a good idea to assign duties while at the contest to each member so they can jump in and help. Ask someone to prep the garnish boxes, another to prepare the sauces, etc. Everyone likes to get in on the action and wants to be involved. It is also a good idea to cross train on various assignments in the event that your garnish man can't make it to a contest, someone else can jump in and get it done.

Some teams will divide each category and let each person be completely responsible for that particular meat. They will supply, prepare, cook, and present the product by themselves. There is no right or wrong way to operate. You should, however, make the determination and assign the responsibilities to avoid any confusion going forward.

If the contest you are entering has any additional categories, first decide if you would like to enter. If so, ask if a teammate would be interested in cooking that entry. This is a great way to involve them in the process and let them have a little of the fun. The difficult part here is trying to stay out of their way and keep your opinions to yourself.

It's also a good idea to keep track of the money that you are spending to fuel this habit called BBQ. Nothing elaborate is needed; a simple accounting book or computer program is sufficient. Try and record everything you purchase for the team and keep a running total. If you are fortunate to have teammates who want to contribute, as I am, it's good to show exactly where the money is going. Entrance fees, contest meats, supplies and equipment, it all adds up in a hurry. It might even be an idea to appoint a team treasurer. Look for a volunteer if possible. You can also use this system to account for any winnings, if your team gets lucky.

# Chapter 8

## BBQ Folks/Good People/Good Friends

Many stories have been written over the years about the good people that you can meet on the BBQ circuit. I had read a lot of those stories over the years before I became a competitor. Stories about people helping each other, offering tips, lending equipment, helping set up, sharing camp food and drink, and even praying when needed. After two seasons on the BBQ circuit, I can tell you that those stories are true.

As many of you already know, I owe the success that we have enjoyed as a team to my good friend and mentor Steve Farin of the I Smell Smoke BBQ team. Steve took me under his wing and showed me the ropes, let me cook with him and still today, offers advice and guidance whenever it is needed. I have gotten to know his parents as well and now it is easy to see why Steve is who he is, good people all around.

In our two short years, we have also become friends with many of the other regulars from around these parts. Teams we have set up next to are the easiest to meet; we always try and introduce ourselves as we are setting up. Many that I have come to know on the various forums that I visit from time to time have also become good friends. I enjoy looking up a team that I have communicated with over the net and speaking to them in person. It is great to put a face with the name.

My only complaint is in the contest setting, there is not a lot of time for visiting. At least, this has been my experience. It seems that when on site at a contest, we are always busy with something. The ideal situation is arriving at the contest site very early on Friday, get set up, get your prep work finished, then you might have a few minutes to walk around and visit. That is, of course, if the folks you are trying to visit have time to speak with you. I don't like to walk into someone's camp when they are trying to prep their meat, lest we be accused of shigging.

After we get our big meats loaded into the cooker and get it somewhat stable, we will take a stroll around as a team and visit with some of our friends. I think many times this is my favorite time at a contest. Most of the crowd has gone; it is just the cooks and the smokers. We wander about with a cold drink and shoot the breeze. Toss in some nice weather and you have got yourself a perfect evening.

There is also another time that I like to visit, that being late Friday night. I do not sleep very well when I am on the road and wound up in a contest, so I will usually wander around the contest grounds after the rest of the team nests up for the night. I will keep stopping back to make sure our cooker is doing what I've asked it to do, but for the most part, this too is a relaxing time for me. The cooks are up tending their cookers and fires and all are very willing to engage anyone that comes by in a discussion about BBQ or anything else for that matter. It is a great time to exchange ideas, tell lies, embellish stories and just BS. Good fun, good people.

Aside from those times, we do not get much time to visit. Saturday morning I am busy with sauces, chicken, ribs and finishing the big meats. We prep the boxes and sometimes we will even cook breakfast. With the first turn in is usually due at 12:00, the morning usually rolls by pretty quickly. After the last box is sent to the judges, we begin to break everything down. Clean and wash the equipment. Cool the cookers, pack the leftovers, load the trailer, well, you get the picture. Most times we just get loaded up and it is time to head to the awards, every once in a while, we get a few minutes to sit down before the ceremony, but not too often. After the awards, a few handshakes, then its head for home, a hot shower and something to eat that isn't BBQ, anything but BBQ.

At first I thought we were doing something wrong, we were not managing our time properly. Then I would see the posts on the forums, "sorry I didn't get around to see everyone," or something like this. Others have the same problem; they are busy at the contest with the contest. It is for this reason that I propose a KCBS sanctioned meet and greet. All teams are invited, we have a huge area reserved, teams arrive early Friday, cook all night, then on Saturday at 12:00, we have a giant picnic, everyone brings a dish.

We sit around and kibitz, eat, drink, and be merry, then at 5:00, we pack up and head for home, with our designated driver of course. No contest, no trophies, just for fun. Sounds like a good time to me.

I have almost forgotten to mention two of the very best, my good friends, Tuffy Stone and Jack MacDavid. The truth be told, neither one of these guys has any idea who I am or who are those guys? At a contest, they are just like your friend. I have had the pleasure of speaking to both from time to time and found them both to be very personable. They are always very friendly and will go the extra mile to help anyone they can. While I was at a contest in New Jersey, I saw Jack giving hands-on advice to a first time team that had set up next to him. In addition to being nice guys, these two are both very good BBQ cooks. Tuffy and his team won nine Grand Championships last season and Jack has done it all from winning many Grands, to appearing on TV along side of Bobby Flay on the Food Network.

In a contest, these two are just a couple of the cooks, or so it seems. What I find extremely impressive is, on Saturday, late morning, along about 11:00 or so, when we are up to our elbows in alligators, you will see them. They will come past each and every site wishing the teams' good luck. The thing to keep in mind is these are two of the guys that everyone is trying to beat. They come by with a smile and a wave, "good luck today fellows!" Very impressive in my book.

Last October at Dover we were lucky enough to take reserve Grand Champion, the past two years the contest was won by Tuffy and his team Cool Smoke. As soon as the awards presentation was over, we were still reeling from the shock, the very first person to walk up and offer his congratulations was my good friend, Tuffy Stone.

# Chapter 9

## Selecting your team name

This is perhaps the most enjoyable part of the entire process. There are many ways to cover this topic. The best advice I can offer is take your time and have some fun. Begin by looking around at various contests and searching the various web sites/forums to get a feel for the names that are out there, and I mean some are really out there.

Some of the names remind me of the titles of porn movies, not that I am familiar with porn movies, but with the way one is bombarded with Internet junk mail these days, one can't help but be exposed to such things. As an example, Romancing the Bone, as a take off from the movie Romancing the Stone. Well, you get the idea. The same line of thinking has gone into the names for BBQ teams. Dr. Porkinstein, The Smokepranos, Butt a Bing BBQ, The Porkshank Redemption and it just rolls on from here. You can see how I could have some fun coming up with a list of names.

Make a list with all of the possibilities. Try to keep in mind something that could personalize your name and or team. Anything to add a little interest to the name will be good. Check the existing team lists from time to time and scratch off names already in use.

One thing to keep in mind here is that BBQ contests are family events. The festivals and fairgrounds where the contests are held attract children and adults of all ages. Please keep this fact in mind when choosing a team name and or your team banner artwork. Try and stay away from any "off color" references or illustrations.

While you are thinking things over, get the opinions from others, even if you don't pay them any attention, like I do. It makes them feel like they were involved. Once you have driven yourself half crazy with team names, look them over and develop a short list. Also, think about the possibilities of a logo to go with your new name, if you can. If not, no big deal, the logo designers out there are very creative and will help you design your own.

As you get close to choosing the final name, I would suggest a Google search be conducted. Here you may find out if your chosen name is being used as a team name or for any other reason that could be an issue in the future. Better safe than sorry.

Finally, make that big decision, then tell the others the name, remember, you're the boss, and a BBQ team is not a democracy. It's a dictatorship, at least until there's a coup or a mutiny. The best part is, other than the expense of your banner, if you don't like the name down the road, you can always change. It's not written in stone.

Be creative when you design your logo and banner. The injection of a little humor is always a great icebreaker. We added a disclaimer to our banner in small print along the bottom (see below). While at a contest, we like to watch the reaction of folks as they walk by. Many look at the banner, never read the disclaimer, and just walk on. It is, after all, in small print. Then there are the ones that do. You can watch as someone reads then begins to laugh. They then nudge their friends and before you know it you have a group standing there laughing and pointing. Many times they will walk up and begin a conversation, asking "where IS Street Maryland?" Great fun.

*Members of "Who Are Those Guys?" Team (left to right): Bob Zengel, Erich Schmitt, Al Smith, George Hensler, and Jo Ann Hensler.*

### Disclaimer:

No animal was harmed unnecessarily in the creation of this BBQ team. The chicken and pig depicted on our banner are professionals and were only acting, they were not harmed in any way. The chicken is actually from Street Maryland and the pig knows damn well who we are.

# Chapter 10

### Cooking Skills

For purposes of this lesson, we are going to assume you already know HOW to cook reasonably good BBQ. In the event that you feel you could use a little improvement or tuning up, I will offer the following suggestions.

The best way to see what others are doing in the competitive arena is to attend a BBQ class. There are many classes offered around the country for competitive BBQ cooking. Many of the top and most successful teams offer classes on cooking a full load of competition meat. Some offer the class as a two-day event, just like a contest and will walk you through everything from meat prep to box building. Encourage others who are interested in the team to attend as well. The price tag for some of these classes may seem a bit steep, but the benefits far outweigh the cost if you are serious about starting a team. Pay attention and take good notes and you will move months ahead on the BBQ learning curve.

Spend time on the various BBQ bulletin boards. Most have searchable archives. Use the search capabilities to research cooking methods for the various contest meats. You will find threads on suggestions for add on categories as well. Many of the boards have regular contributions from proven Champions and BBQ legends. Some have recipe and technique sections. You will find as many opinions and methods as there are BBQ cooks. Some guys make all their own sauces and rubs. Some guys cook fast, others slow; they are all represented somewhere on the net or in available cookbooks. Research, read, practice, repeat.

I recently came across what I consider to be one of the most detailed accounts for preparing competition chicken that I have ever found. It is right there on the net for all to see and was written by one of the leading chicken cooks on the circuit. It is definitely worth the read, here is the site: http://www.thepickledpig.com/howtobbq/chicken/chicken.cfm

I would also suggest taking the classes to become a certified judge. Classes sponsored by KCBS are held all around the Country throughout the year. The KCBS web site is a great place to check for classes and their availability. Sign up for the class and become a judge. Two reasons here. One is to get more experience around the contest venue by volunteering to judge a contest and to see what kind of product others are turning in. The second is to familiarize yourself with the rules and requirements for the competitors at a KCBS contest and to see exactly what the judges are looking for. Both will serve to improve your knowledge of what is expected in a KCBS contest.

Cook BBQ whenever you can. You will be having it for breakfast, lunch and dinner. Early on, the *fam* will think they are in heaven, "Mmmmmm BBQ, bring it on." If possible, prepare the meat as you might in a contest. Keep good notes on your cooks. Record what seasonings you used, the sauces, cook times, internal temps, outside temps, weather conditions, any shred of information that may affect the final outcome of the product. After you sample your food, have others taste it and get their opinion. Make notes, review the notes, then review them again, decide on changes to make, then cook again. When you think you are finished, start all over again. You will know you are getting close to being finished when the kids come to the dinner table and say, "yuck, brisket AGAIN."

Establish a base line for your cooking procedure. You need to be consistent with your method so that the final product remains the same. By taking good notes and recording your every step, you should be able to maintain a consistent product. Once you have that down and decide to make a change, go slow. Do not change too many steps or ingredients at one time. Work slowly and record the outcome. Good note taking along with honest and thorough evaluation after the cook are essential in producing a consistent product time after time.

Get a 'feel' for your meat. I know, that sounds like a statement that should not be made on a family show, but I am serious, feel your meat. Learn the difference in how the meat feels when you are sliding in the temperature probe as the temperature rises. How does the meat feel when it's done? How about when you are pulling and or slicing, does it feel mushy? dry? tender? hard? Learn to know what you are looking for; again, it is attention to detail.

Taste your product along the way, before you sauce it, and again before it goes into the box. Is the meat moist, flavorful, does it need anything. How is the texture, the tenderness? Should you add salt, a dash of cayenne?

Taste your sauce before you apply it to your product. Does it need anything? How about after you sauce? Have you allowed the sauce to set? How does it pair with the meat? Would the overall product benefit from a last minute dash of anything? If so, by all means add it. You do not get a second chance with the judges.

Remember, you are cooking for the judges, not the family or yourself. You will want to find out what the judges are looking for in the area you are competing. Talk to other cooks while taking classes or while at a contest. When starting out, my advice would be not to stray too far from the norm. A contest is not a good place to experiment.

Look around, many contests will have a backyard or tailgate contest in conjunction with the regular KCBS event. These contests typically cook only one meat, usually chicken or ribs. They don't take a huge investment to participate in. The plus side is you can get a feeling for the contest experience. This can be very helpful to see for sure if you and your prospective team members really want to get involved in this madness called competitive cooking. They are also a lot of fun. The downside is you expose yourself to becoming addicted to this crazy "sport." Remember, you have been warned.

While you are involved in your test cooking operation, be sure to note the results of the sauces and rubs that you want to use. Some teams use over the counter products, others make their own, still others use a combination. Whichever way you go, make sure you have a reliable source for obtaining the materials you need. Be sure you always have enough on hand to accommodate any test cooks or contests that are scheduled.

While at a contest, offer some of your extras to the surrounding teams for their opinion. If they offer, sample their product. How does it compare to your submission? Make a mental note, then check the results, see how they did. Match their score to yours.

While you are at it, pay attention to the source of the meats you are cooking. Again, make notes and look at the meat you are buying. Are you satisfied with the outcome, your final result? In my opinion, an inferior piece of meat going into the cooker is not going to improve when it comes out; no matter how slowly it cooks. Develop a relationship with your butcher, whether it's at the local discount box store, or around the corner at the neighborhood meat market. Explain to them what you are after, what you are looking for in a certain cut of meat. Don't just take what they hand you, look it over and make sure it looks like a cut that you want to cook. Try to get the best product you can to start with, even if this means going to several suppliers to gather all of the meat needed for a contest. You will not regret any time spent securing a better product to begin with. Then it's only up to you not to screw it up after that.

# Chapter 11

## Transportation

Transportation is a key issue. Sounds like a political statement doesn't it? In this case, it is not political, but very important, contrary to most political statements. How will you get all of the necessary gear to and from the contest venue? Will the cooker you have selected be able to be moved without using a crane or developing a hernia? Where will the gear be stowed between contests? Will the supplies stay dry during transport? If you are considering a trailer, is it big enough? Do you have a beefy enough tow vehicle? What about fuel costs? All are very valid questions that need to be addressed. In other words, transportation is a key issue.

If you are in the position and have the funding, I would suggest a heavy-duty ¾ ton pickup, extended cab, 4-wheel drive and a trailer towing package. A nice 15-18 foot enclosed trailer with a rear loading ramp and side access would be a nice tow vehicle. If the trailer was set up as a mobile kitchen, included air conditioning and had a couple of bunks, you would be all set.

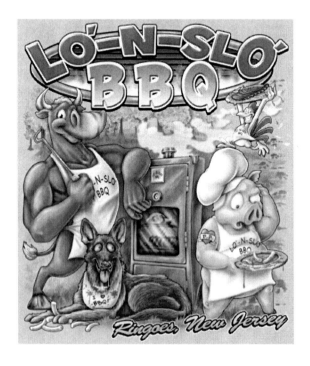

Unfortunately, most of us cannot go out and purchase a complete competition rig before our first contest. Reality and family responsibilities dictate another, more conservative approach.

If you have not decided on a cooker yet, I would recommend giving the method of moving from home to contest a large amount of consideration in the decision making process. Nothing would be worse than getting your new cooker up and running, then realizing you don't have any way to get it to your first contest.

I would suggest looking around to see what you and your teammates already have at your disposal. A truck capable of hauling some extra weight and or a trailer of some type is great to have. Of course, you could always rent a trailer and a truck for your run to the contest site, but I think it makes more sense to own them.

An enclosed trailer is ideal because your equipment can stay dry and safe when locked inside the trailer. If the trailer is big enough, you could even use the interior at the contest site to get in out of the weather if the situation arises. This trailer also can serve as a dry place to store your contest equipment in between events.

All of this discussion about trailers only serves to point out one way to get around. You do not need a trailer to compete. A pickup or two can be more than enough space to get you and your equipment to your first contest. Again, initially, I would stress working to keep the costs to operate down to a manageable level. At least until you get a couple of contests under your belt and can decide for yourself what you will need to compete.

# Chapter 12

### Equipment selection

Make your lists and check them twice. Go over your lists and begin to gather the needed supplies and equipment (see item list). Try to gather gradually, to lessen the financial impact on your wallet. There are numerous BBQ supply stores on the Internet. Charcoal, wood chunks, rubs and sauces can all be ordered online if you do not have a source near by. You could do a Google search or my suggestion would be Hawgeyes BBQ, www.hawgeyes-bbq.com. They have a great selection and offer fast service.

Some of the equipment you may already have. Some can serve double duty between the home kitchen and the contest box. I would suggest keeping this arrangement to a minimum. It never fails, when you get to the contest, the needed item is back home in the kitchen. Keep items devoted to BBQ in the contest box whenever possible.

I suggest keeping a list of contest items in the front of your contest notebook. It is also a good idea to keep a running list while at the contests. In it, you can note if you discover an item you would like to bring along next time. If you empty a jar of rub, make a note to purchase a fresh supply before the next event. It is also a good idea to look around and make sure everything you are bringing is actually needed and is used. If you find that an item is not useful, leave it home and lighten the load.

Stay organized. Try and keep your site as neat and organized as possible. It is much easier to work in a neat kitchen. It is also much safer. Plastic tubs with lids make great storage containers and can be stacked on top of each other. They also provide a dry area when the lids are used. Organize your supplies into their own storage container. Labeling the boxes helps with locating an item and is also convenient for returning them to their proper place when you are finished.

Make provisions for comfort. Most contests involve an overnight stay. Unless you are very skilled, lucky, or carefree, someone from the team will be staying near the cooker during the overnight hours. Make sure you have a cot, sleeping bag and pillow to facilitate at least a modicum of rest.

Another item to be sure to keep on hand is a well-stocked first aid kit. If you use materials from the kit, be sure to note it on your contest list to be replaced. Locate your kit as you would your fire suppression equipment, in a prominent place. Make sure all of the others on the team know the location of each of these items in the event they are needed in an emergency.

Tylenol, Ibuprofen, Tums etc. are must haves in the contest box. Another handy item to bring along is some Gold Bond ointment or powder in the event that any chaffing issues arise. Take it from me; there is no quicker way to ruin your day.

Disposable latex gloves are very handy and you should have plenty on hand. Change them often. Do not cross contaminate. Keep a bottle of anti-bacterial disinfectant with bleach on hand to wipe off work surfaces. Buy paper towels by the gross—you are going to need them.

A portable weather radio with a warning alarm is a piece of equipment you can have with you for years and never use. However, there may come that one time when you are glad that you have it. BBQ contest are usually held during the summer months when fast-moving thunderstorms can occur. A warning about impending severe weather will be very helpful in prevention of equipment loss or damage, not to mention personal safety.

## GYPSY BBQ

# COMPETITION TEAM
### MILLVILLE, NJ

# Chapter 13

**Contest ZZZZZ's, Necessary or overrated?**

During my short time around the BBQ circuit, one aspect, in my opinion, is the most widely varied. The methods and means are almost as different as are the many team names and signage. Of course, I am speaking of team sleeping arrangements.

A walk around any contest site on a Friday afternoon will give the astute observer a good idea on what is to come. Of course, teams with travel trailers or campers are flying in the upper strata of snoozers. Lights, private rest rooms, heaters and or air conditioners, showers, beds, electric give these lucky folks the feeling like they are just cooking out in the back yard. Another huge advantage to this type of set up is having room to carry all of your gear without too much trouble. Bad weather, no problemo, just build your box in the kitchen, no worry about any high winds or rain. This set up is generally in the minority at most contests that I have seen.

Next you have the tent dwellers. If site space permits, some teams will pitch tents of varying shapes and sizes in order to facilitate a little shuteye. This is a great idea if you have a family and or young children with your group. This arrangement allows some privacy and creates a great space for kids to bunk down, somewhat away from the fray.

Another group deserves mention, although I wonder how they can even exist. These are the automated cookers sometimes known as motel guests. You will see their sites late Friday night, all set up, cookers smoking, not a soul in sight. One would assume that they arrive back on site at the appropriate time to begin the morning cook but who knows; perhaps they have that phase of the operation on automatic pilot as well. All I know is, there is no way I could even begin to sleep in a motel while I was wondering if everything was going as it should back at the contest site, 5 miles away. I would be a nervous wreck, and surely I could never find the Z zone, no matter how many pigs I counted.

The next bunch I like to refer to as the zombie Q'ers. This is the group that never sleeps. They arrive early Friday, work all day around their camp, and then stay up all night stoking their fires or wandering the contest grounds yaking with the other cooks. They will even go as far as to interrupt others when they are trying to sleep. The walking dead don't even sit long enough to take a nap. I don't know how they do it. I am guessing they really enjoy what they are doing, or they are 'in fact' zombies, or they have a large supply of Red Bull stashed somewhere.

The Rube Goldberg gang is next. This group will use tarps, blankets, plastic sheeting, cardboard, just about anything they can find to construct a shelter for the night. Sometimes the result is successful, other times, not. Some look like they are built to last, while others look as though a stiff sneeze would knock it over. Either way, I believe that they do achieve the desired effect, whether it be privacy or darkness, which ever they are after. As long as the wind doesn't blow too hard.

The car sleepers are another very popular group at most BBQ contests. A walk through the parking area of any contest on Friday night will find many autos with their windows steamed like a July night back at the Bengies Drive-in. The difference is, instead of two passionate youths rolling around in the front seat trying to find love, you will probably find some snoring fat guy with a BBQ stain on his shirt sprawled out across the back seat trying to find his bottle of ant-acid. The bigger difference is, you wouldn't mind seeing the first scenario, (maybe bringing back a pleasant memory or two), while a glimpse of the second would easily give you nightmares for months to come, or send you running directly into therapy, or both.

A sub-group to the car sleeper is the slightly more sophisticated, truck sleeper. This is the guy that sleeps in the cargo area of his pick-up, with or without a cap. The guy sleeping with a cap on the truck is not doing too bad, it is almost like a camper. Emphasis on the word ALMOST. The guy sleeping in the cargo area, no cap, in the parking lot, can give the unsuspecting pedestrian quite a jolt when walking by the truck at the same time the sleeping man decides to pass gas. Nuff said.

39

The shift workers. This is a very smooth operation if run properly. Teammates will take turns or shifts watching the cookers and tending the camp throughout the night. When you are off, you can hit the hay or go and play, the choice is yours. This is probably the safest way to ensure a trouble free overnight cook. I cannot explain why we have not explored this as a possibility, perhaps the folks on my team like their sleep too much. Maybe I will put a note into the suggestion box for the upcoming season.

The remaining group, which I feel has the largest contingent, is the gang I refer to as the homeless cookers. To which, we are honored to be members. Very late on Friday night you will see some of them starting to nest up. Some are observed stumbling dreary eyed through the contest grounds carrying cots, pillows and or sleeping bags. Areas are cleared, sometimes cots are erected. Other times reclining chairs are broken out. Many times, you'll see them just curled up on a cooler or an open spot on a trailer. Some can even venture into dream land while sitting upright in a lawn chair. These are the lucky ones in my opinion. The entire scene is eerily similar to a down town park. There you might see a bench sleeper, a ground sleeper, and even a lucky grate sleeper if the outside temps are getting cool.

Our team, as I mentioned is a part of the homeless cookers. We each bring along a cot, sleeping bag and pillow and set up under our easy-up. We will try and arrange it so the cots are away from the prep table so the early rib man (me) doesn't disturb our resting crew attempting to get their beauty sleep. God knows they need all the help they can get. I usually try and set my cot next to the cookers so I can keep an eye on the situation from the bunk.

For me, I erect a cot and lay out my sleeping bag and pillow. I am not a sound sleeper under perfect circumstances. So let's just say at a contest, I am lucky if I can get in a nap. A combination of outside noises, worry about the cooker, and overall contest jitters keep me from falling into a deep sleep. Usually, the rest of the team will bunk down and I will sit up and watch the cookers for a while. Before turning in, I like to take another walk around the contest to see who is still up. This is a great time to meet and greet some folks that are usually busy most other times. I usually stay away from sites where I can hear large amounts of logs being sawed.

Along about 1:30 or 2:00am I will lie down and try to catch some Z's. Sometimes I am successful, sometimes not, but at least I try. My alarm clock chirping at 5:30 reminds me to rise and get the ribs ready to hit the smoke. I usually try and make just enough noise as to wake my slumbering teammates without disturbing the sleepers in the immediate area. Sometimes this necessitates "accidentally" dropping something next to their head, ooops!

Daybreak at a BBQ contest is my favorite time. Just about everyone has

40

# Suggested Items

## Equipment

Smoker Grill Grill tools      _____
Knives/steel      _____
Canopy/EZ up      _____
Water jug      _____
Buckets Wash basins      _____
Work tables      _____
Broom/rake      _____
Dish rags/towels      _____
Cutting board      _____
Flashlight/headlamp      _____
Clock      _____
Meat thermometer      _____
Notebook/pen      _____
Chairs      _____
Extension cords      _____
Coolers/meat/drinks      _____
Coffee pot      _____
Measuring devices/cups/spoons      _____
Assorted kitchen utensils      _____
Tongs, Flippers, Scissors, Utility knife      _____
Containers for mixing sauces      _____
Trash can      _____
Spare cooker parts      _____
Basting brushes      _____
External thermometers      _____
Pots/pans/trays Propane stove/burner      _____
Electric power strips/3 ways      _____
Fire starter/torch/chimney      _____
Fire extinguisher      _____
Bungee cords      _____
Banner/flags      _____
Stereo/CDs/iPod      _____
Clip on lights/extra bulbs      _____
Hose/nozzle      _____
Pot holders/hot gloves      _____
Tool box      _____
Grill brush      _____
Spray bottle      _____
Cambro/cooler      _____
    (for holding finished meats)
First aid kit      _____

## Supplies

Aluminum foil
Aluminum pans/full/half
Bleach
Dish soap
Hand soap
Insect repellant
Paper towels
Plastic ware/cups/plates/etc.
Fuel/charcoal/wood/pellets
Wood chunks/chips
Latex gloves
Matches/lighter
Zip lock bags/assorted sizes
Ice
Plastic wrap
Sun screen
Spare propane bottles
Batteries
Coffee filters
Trash bags
Spray Cleaner
Duct tape
Degreaser spray

_____
_____
_____
_____
_____
_____
_____
_____
_____
_____
_____
_____
_____
_____
_____
_____
_____
_____
_____
_____
_____
_____
_____

## Food Items

Rubs
Contest meats/brisket/ribs/chicken/pork
Sauces
Garnishes
Beer
Drinking water
Sport drinks
Additional seasonings
Camp grub (make it something good)
Coffee/cream/sugar

   _____
   _____
   _____

## Other Stuff

Toilet kit
Extra clothes
Change of shoes/sox
Personal medications
Cell phone/charger
Camera
Hat
Rain gear/mud boots/umbrella
GPS
Laptop
Weather radio w/alarm
Sweatshirt/jacket/coat
Sunglasses
Reading glasses
Gold Bond cream
Aprons
Sleeping bag/cot/pillow

their smokers rolling and the sweet smell is everywhere. A smokey haze hangs over the area sometimes so thick you could cut it with a knife. It is too early for any pedestrians, so the crowd is limited to other cooks moving about without the urgency they will have later in the day. Everyone is generally subdued; no loud music is being played. The heat of the day is in check for a while. Most of the drunks are either passed out or in a stupor. The loudest noise is the occasional tearing of sheet of aluminum foil being used in the cooking process. This must be what it is like in BBQ heaven.

We will put on some coffee and all is well in our little corner of the world. I always leave my cot up after I rise with the intention of getting a chance to lie back down after the ribs are on. In two years, I haven't made it back to the sack a single time. Maybe this year I will.

As the morning inches forward, folks take down their makeshift shelters and begin to roll up their sleeping bags in preparation for the days' activities. As for me, I haven't made it back to my bag; I've got too much to do. I am way behind already and its not even 9:00. I might as well break it down and roll it up; right now it's just in the way. What do you say we amble over to the soup kitchen to see what they are serving for breakfast? Sleep at a contest, definitely overrated in my book. Breakfast at a contest, now that is a necessity. Maybe I'll get lucky and grab a nap after turn-ins and before the awards.

# Chapter 14

**Practice Contest**

I would suggest if at all possible doing a practice run, a complete run through, A to Z, of actual contest conditions. Pick a date that is convenient to all your team members and do a complete contest set up and cook. Pick your turn-in times and have them scheduled as you would in a contest with half an hour in between. Plan backwards to determine when you will begin cooking your meats. At a contest, the average site size is around 20 x 20, but sizes do vary. Use this as a guideline when planning your space. Erect your canopies, tables, cookers and grills. Set up your lights so you can see at night. Do you have enough cords and lights packed?

If possible, cooler your meats and do the prep work in the site you have set up. This will give you a good idea if you have gathered everything you will need at your first contest. It will also give a good trial run for cooking all four categories' at once. Go through the entire process including preparing the boxes. After you have written a check for an entry fee is not the time to try and construct your first box. Keep good notes and record any problems encountered. Invite some friends over to act as judges and taste the

**Competition BBQ Team**

food you have prepared. Make a party out of it. Post pictures of your boxes and ask the other cooks for their opinions. Again, most are willing to help a new guy get started.

While doing your mock-up or at a contest, keep a journal. Assign a team member to make journal entries. Have them note the steps taken to each piece of meat. Record what rubs and seasonings are used, cooker temps, the times when meats are inserted into the cooker. Note the temperatures during the cook along with what time they were taken. If foiling, what time and temp. Pay attention, you'd be surprised, when you try and remember things during your post cook debriefing, how quickly you can forget.

When you have finished go back and review. Do you need to change or did you like the result? Refer to the notes during practice and at the next cook. Most experienced competition BBQ cooks do not record their every action. They know what they are doing. You are new. I recommend this step until you are completely comfortable with your competition Queing skills.

Go through the entire cook, clean up, and pack everything away. It would be a good idea here to pack the vehicles you plan to use for transportation to and from the contest site. Any thing you can do to make yourself ready, with the ultimate goal of reducing the stress and confusion associated with your first contest run is worth doing. The more relaxed you are, the more enjoyable the entire experience will be. The more enjoyable and relaxed you are, the better chance you have to concentrate on producing the best product that you can.

# Chapter 15

### Chicken, chicken and more chicken—the lonely world of a chicken man

This past winter, I have been cooking chicken thighs. Each week I have prepped and cooked approximately 16 pieces of chicken, a rough estimate would say that I have cooked 128 thighs. I am not sure that number is correct, but it is pretty darn close. That's a lot of chicken.

My wife is about to have me committed. She feels I need professional help. Perhaps on a University level, at the very least some type of a support group. Maybe she is right. I know I need help with my chicken, judging by recnt results.

I have been trying to refine my chicken cooking technique and procedure. Some weeks I have been very happy and think I about got it down, then bammo, the next week, another gremlin jumps into the mix, and it feels like I am back to square one.

What follows are some random thoughts of a half crazed chicken man concerning my journey down Yard Bird Lane. I will try and note the good and the bad. I hope there will be something that you will be able to use, should you decide to examine your own chicken prowess.

If you are going to practice cooking chicken, do just that. Do not attempt to work on ribs and or brisket at the same time. An even worse idea is to try and clean the garage while cooking your chicken. Chicken is a short cook as you well know, distractions, even small ones can have disastrous results. As I learned during week six, while tending a brisket flat and two racks of spares I had going with the chicken, I neglected the chicken rack for a couple of minutes during a crucial time and ended up burning the skin. After saucing when I presented to the Judge, (my wife), she quipped, "that's got to be the worst-looking chicken that you have ever cooked." Just what you want to hear after cooking 96 pieces, and I thought I was getting somewhere.

Take good notes. Weekends around my house are very busy. I am always behind schedule and trying to cram 12 hours of tasks into an 8-hour schedule. Even after lighting the smoker, there is a fair amount of work to get your chicken ready to be cooked. As I am rushing around, I usually end up recording my cook times and temps on the back of an envelope or a piece of scrap paper, not a good idea. Today, week eight, I found myself reading scribbled notes on several envelopes trying to make sense out of what I had already tried. This is not what I would call efficient.

Find someone who likes chicken thighs and get them on speed dial. The first week, we had them for dinner. Week 2, they ate them as an appetizer. By week 3, the family wanted no more and began to lock the door when I went outside to check on the cooker. Not very pleasant in mid winter. The kids won't even look at a chicken thigh—they are about filled up on all things BBQ.

Then I found out teammate and neighbor Erich just loves chicken thighs. I called him and he came right up and even took what was left home as a carry out. This was a nice arrangement for a week or so. I then began to notice on Sunday afternoons, Erich was not taking my calls. It seems everyone today has caller ID. When driving by on Sundays, he wouldn't even look over! I bagged the thighs up and drove them to his house, but no one was home. I thought I just saw him drive by?

I am not sure, but I would swear that I saw the curtains move when I got out of the truck, and now that I think about it, all of their cars were there… hmmmmmm….

Last week teammate Mike came by when I was midway through my new procedure. He looked and watched as anyone would while observing a madman at work. He then began to ask a few questions to be able to get a handle on what I was doing. I noticed as I began to explain that I was get-

ting into way too much detail. My arms were flailing about and I could feel sweat on my forehead as I described my latest idea. It was only 40 degrees outside. I couldn't see them, but I am sure that my eyes were wide and occasionally spinning around in their sockets. I was tossing around words like oyster, fat layer, fat pockets, excess skin, bite through and rubberized. I am not sure all of these terms are officially associated with chicken but I was reciting them like the Gettysburg Address.

Could it be, I was over thinking this, after all, it was just chicken. But, after spending so much quality time with my friend the yard bird, I felt I had to explain, had to give them the respect that I felt they deserved, we had spent so much time together. I feel I have become intimate with the thigh. Placed into spiritual context, the thigh and I have become one. We are operating in accord. I have chicken Karma so to speak, chicken harmony. My favorite song is now Louis Jordan, "Ain't nobody here but us chickens." I have been searching the Internet for an alarm clock with the sound of a rooster crowing. I am not sure, but while shaving this morning I thought I saw some pinfeathers in the sink basin.

Maybe my wife is right, maybe I lost my mind. I have been consumed with cooking chicken thighs. I did 15 today and have another 16 ready to go tomorrow. I plan to put them on after I take a ride to pick up another load of; you guessed it, chicken thighs. As I was watching the smoke roll this afternoon it hit me, this chicken cookin is a lonely deal.

I called Mike, and got the answering machine, cell and house, dam caller ID. I got a hold of Erich, he said he would love to come up but he had to water his lawn. That is funny, I never heard of watering your lawn in mid March and besides, it was raining. The kids all went to their friends' house for dinner after they saw me lighting up. As for my chicken and me, I'll keep pecking away, (pun intended), maybe someday I'll get the hang of it. In the meantime, I wonder if that new guy that just moved in down the street likes thigh meat?

# Chapter 16

## An intervention of sorts

I can no longer write about c*****n, or any poultry product for that matter, at least that's what my counselor has told me. I must cut the bond, return to reality. All at once too, its sort of like cold t****y, I am not allowed to use that word either, you know, associated poultry products and all. Yes, that's right, my counselor, well, I call her a group leader. I have joined a support group that I found online. It is a small group, as I am the only current member. I mainly joined to just silence my wife, I really don't need it, at least I thought I didn't.

It all started one weekend in March, the day began just like any other Sunday morning. I went outside to light the smoker and get her up to temperature. After getting the fire started I went to the outside refrigerator to get the c*****n, I mean the meat that I had prepared to smoke that day. When I opened the fridge, the meat was gone, vanished. I was hot, I could feel myself begin to sweat, my heart was racing, had I left it out all night? It was over 40 degrees; if it was out on the counter I was doomed. Perhaps the inside fridge, in a severe panic I rushed into the kitchen.

As I opened the door, the entire kitchen was filled with my friends and family, and they were all looking at me with pity in their eyes, I knew I was in trouble. My birthday is not until December, this could not be a surprise party, what the heck was going on. "George, we need to talk", my wife began, and it was down hill from there. I think the terminology here is intervention. You know, you have seen it on TV before for drug addicts and alcoholics, they happen all the time.

To my knowledge, this is a first for a supposed poultry addiction. Each of the people standing in the kitchen were clutching some type of non poultry item for me to smoke. There was salmon, oysters, almonds, ABT's, one neighbor offered a pan of salt. Teammate/neighbor Erich brought along a cigar, I guessed for me to smoke. Later that afternoon, in private, Erich confided that he HAD been home that Sunday that I was knocking on his door, go figure.

They all took turns explaining the why-fors and how-to's as to why they though I had lost control and how sick they were of you know what. Each attempting to make a case as to the reason I should spend time smoking their particular offering this fine Sunday afternoon. All except for Erich, the cigar apparently was for him, he announced he was going out to the smoker to have a beer and light up. As he passed by, he whispered, "I am with you on this," and that fast he was gone, leaving me alone in my defense of the angry mob.

At first, I fought them; my group leader says I was in denial. Besides, I thought to myself, I had a couple of bags of thighs in the freezer, as soon as the circus left town, I'd break them out, do a quick thaw, then get them in the smoke. Not to be, during my wife's portion of the show, she held up a large trash bag containing my former friends. She told me she removed every one from both freezers and was throwing them out!

Noooooooo! I screamed. Nooooooooooooo! That's when it hit me, I had hit rock bottom. I saw the light, I had been possessed. I felt like the weight of a giant c*****n had been lifted from my back. Most will tell you cannot begin to recover until you bottom out and admit your problem, its all included in the ten step program I am now involved with.

Ms. Feather, my counselor, said the first step of my recovery program is a public admission of my problem. I am here now to do just that, as I scream from the valley to the mountaintops; "my name is George Hensler, and I am a chickaholic."

I am not sure, but I think she made that word up. You know how these Internet self help outfits are, I am not sure Ms. Feather has any real certification, in fact, I am not even sure she's a she or if her last name is really Feather, but I won't go there. In the interest of marital harmony between Jo and I, I will go along with the "program," certification or not. I will stay with it even if I find out that Ms. Feather is some 21 year old male computer geek from India named Bharat. To this cause, I am committed.

I also discovered that it is not a good idea to contact your health insurance carrier on April 1st to ask them if chickaholic counseling is covered under your current plan. That is, of course you enjoy being laughed at and hung up on, I know I don't. I guess this is what they call the shame of addiction.

Another step according to Ms. Feather is revealing the depth of the problem. Sort of like the Festivus airing of grievances. Believe me, if I had any inkling that my wife ever read this book, I would be skipping this part, but here goes, to the best of my knowledge, here are the figures, please don't tell her.

Average of 15 thighs per week for 12 weeks-180 pieces
Approximately 3 thighs to the pound- 60 pounds
60 pounds of thighs- .99 per pound- $59.40
Fuel to run back and forth gathering meat and supplies- $40.00
12 loads of charcoal- $3.50 per - $42.00
Sauce, marinade, rub- $11.00 per week- $132.000
Thighs taste tested by me- 48 (not good for my figure)

Modifications to cooker in an attempt to improve product- $250.00
1 hour prep- 4 hours cooking for each batch- 60 hours total time commitment @ 15.00 per hour - $900.000
Total monetary outlay for materials $523.40
Total expenditure- $1,423.40
WOW, I had no idea.

I suppose Ms. Feather has a point, when you look at it this way, it certainly appears that I have lost something besides 60 man hours and over $500 clams; my dignity. But, I am here to tell you I have cast off those chains. No longer will my life be dominated and ruled by a small white bird that scratches around the yard looking for worms.

I am taking control, I have been in the coop long enough, I now have feelings again of want and longing. I have the desire to cook something else besides the C word. I am again alive. What about a nice brisket or a rack of spares, now, doesn't that just inspire a warm and fuzzy feeling inside your tummy?

I am glad to be well, although never cured; I know I will always have a struggle on my hands. Set backs and slip ups are common in today's world. Just look around, there is a Kentucky Fried or a Chick- Fil- A on just about every corner these days. It's not an easy gig being a recovering chickaholic. I look forward to the challenge, taking it one day at a time. If I start jonesin for some white meat and need to take the edge off, I'll just grab a couple of McNuggets, that's about as far from a piece of c*****n that you can get.

Feelings, I have them again and I am glad. Up until the intervention, I could describe only one feeling. The feeling you get when you bite into thigh #179, and the skin pulls off the top of the meat, won't bite through, and falls like a piece of rubber onto the first of your three chins while sauce droplets careen down the front of your new shirt. I can sum that feeling up in one word, 'sickening!'

# Chapter 17

## Site Safety

I equate setting up a BBQ site to a combination of camping and kitchen design. When you arrange your cook-site, you keep certain thoughts in mind. From the camping aspect, observe everything you can to assure a safe environment. You will be cooking, relaxing, and possibly sleeping within your site. Keep all of these multiple uses in mind while setting up. Along the lines of kitchen design, you are in effect, designing a kitchen for which to operate for a day or two. Keep the word efficiency in mind. Make your set up with a working triangle in mind, just as you would when laying out a kitchen design.

Use common sense when setting up your site. Watch overhead for power lines if erecting high banners or flagpoles. If you are driving stakes to anchor canopies, be sure it is permissible by the contest organizers and also check for any underground cables or pipes.

If you are using canopies, it is a good idea to anchor the corners down in case of strong winds. Most come with a set of stakes which are often times too small in my opinion. Larger more efficient stakes can be found at hardware or camping supply stores. If you are on a hard surface such as asphalt or concrete it is understood that your stakes are useless. Some teams have weights that are used to tie down the corners of the canopies. If you have coolers or vehicles nearby, they can be used as corner tie-down anchors. We use old 5-gallon drywall buckets, filled with water. They offer enough weight to do the job and, after the contest, they can be emptied, stacked and transported with relative ease when compared to heavy bulky weights.

Make sure you have a working fire extinguisher in your site and everyone knows where it is. This is a requirement at most contests. When positioning your smokers and grills, make sure the area is level and out of the way of anticipated foot traffic. Look around for other vehicles parked in the area and be sure to keep a safe distance when locating your cookers.

Always carry a first aid kit. Be sure if any team member needs any personal medications to have them on hand or at the very least be aware of the situation. Emergency contact info including important cell phone numbers for each team member is good to have. You never know.

Some teams will use a large turkey fryer burner to heat water for clean up. If you are using a set-up like this, make sure the connections are tight and the LP tank is located away from any direct heat source. Most of the contest venues are very tight for space and there is a lot of equipment and vehicles crammed into a very small area.

Portable lanterns, stoves, space heaters, and hot water heaters use the small propane bottles. Care must be used here as well. Remember, you are in a small area with a large concentration of combustible and flammable materials. Also present are a large number of people in varying degrees of sobriety, and then there are the folks attending the contest. Use caution when lighting, using and storing this equipment. Again, there is a fair amount of activity in the site while it is dark and visibility is limited, so keep this in mind when positioning equipment. Flashlights and the newer strap-on headlamps are good tools to have on hand.

When stringing lights for effect or so you can see at night, pay attention to the cords. Remember folks will be walking all around during the night. Do not lay cords across areas where they might be tripped over. Also, be sure electrical connections and cords are not in an area that will get wet either by rain or by runoff.

One of the required utensils to have on hand at a BBQ contest are sharp knifes. Care must be exercised when transporting, storing and using these items. For transporting, I would suggest a knife case. They are available with hard or soft covers. This makes safe transportation a breeze and also protects

the cutting edge. Cases are available on line and at some of the kitchen supply stores around town. At the very least, sheaths are necessary if you do not have a case. Transport and store your knives by themselves. Most importantly, do not toss your knifes into a box, unprotected, along with other assorted utensils. This can be very harmful to the cutting edge and even more harmful to your teammates' fingers as he roots through the pile looking for a wisk for the sauce and finds your boning knife blade.

While you are at a contest, be sure to use common sense when setting up your site. Do not leave valuable items around and out in the open, especially when you are walking around the grounds or are bedding down for the night. Items like expensive knives, wallets, pocketbooks, iPods, and stereos can be lifted very quickly and easily. Use a locking vehicle to store valuable items. Just be sure to use the LOCKS. Most competitors watch out for each other but, many venues are open to the public all night long and you never know who or what will come wandering through. I have even heard of competitors having their meats stolen from their cookers.

Contests are usually held in the summer months. Care must be taken to protect you and your team from the sun. If you have erected canopies, hopefully you will be operating underneath in the shade. Sunscreen, sunglasses and large brimmed hats are suggested for protection from the sun's rays. While you are busy with contest prep, oftentimes you do not realize the power of the sun. It is good to get a jump here and apply sunscreens in the morning before you get too busy.

While you and your teammates are busy with prep, cooking and turn-ins, it is very easy to become distracted. As the heat of the day climbs along with the heat from the grills and cookers, things can get a little warm. Be sure to have plenty of drinking water on hand. It is also advisable to have some type of sports drink available. If the heat is going to be an issue, it is very important that team members ingest the proper fluids—not all beer—to prevent dehydration and or heat stroke.

Police your area before you leave. Be sure you have properly disposed of all gray water, trash, hot ash and coals. If a hot coal bin is not nearby, a disposable aluminum pan works great. It is much safer than moving through a crowded fair ground, dodging pedestrians, while holding a hot drawer filled with glowing red coals on the way to the barrel on the other side of the park. Put your coals into the pan, then fill with water. Make sure all coals and fires are out before leaving your site.

# Chapter 18

## The Judges and Organizers

If you're planning to enter the world of competition BBQ cooking and would like to know as much as you can about the process, the logical place to begin would be to become a certified KCBS judge. At the risk of sounding redundant, I feel that this is almost a required step in the learning process.

By taking the class, you will learn the judging procedures, contest rules, and what the judges are told to look for when tasting your product. You also become certified which allows you to apply to any KCBS contest in the Country, and to be considered a judge for a particular contest or event. After judging 30 or more contests, you can then apply to be considered as a Certified Master Judge.

All contests attempt to use active current certified judges. The judges at a contest are advised not to fraternize with the teams at the contest to which they are judging. This is prohibited by KCBS rules. Before the judges' orientation they can visit briefly with teams, afterwards they cannot. After the judging process is complete, they can fraternize with anyone.

The judges are all volunteers. If you see a judge in the event area after the judging is complete, be sure to thank them for their time and effort. Without them, there would be no contest. In this same line, if you are a participant in one of the various BBQ forums, be sure to keep in mind the fact that the judges are VOLUNTEERS. Direct any complaints and concerns about judging issues to the KCBS contest reps for resolution before screaming, crying and whining on a public forum. Remember, judges have feelings too.

Be sure to acknowledge the organizers and volunteers, especially if it has been a good experience. A simple thank you, or the offer of a cold drink or a bite to eat goes a long way. You may even consider dropping the Chairperson a thank you note the following week. If there were issues or problems that you feel need addressing, make them aware of the situation, along with the offer of a possible solution. Just be sure to thank them for their efforts. Remember, without the organizers and volunteers, we would not have a contest. Those two words, thank you, carry a lot of weight; don't be afraid to use them.

# Chapter 19

## Your First Contest

You have made your decision and are looking forward to the contest season. It is time to make the hardest step of all, entering your first contest. Check the Internet for a contest schedule. Try and find events that are close to your home base and spread out throughout the season. For your first, if possible, try and pick an event that may not draw a huge field of teams. Don't overdo it and sign up for too many out of the gate. Pick a couple and apply. That is the easy part.

Once your application has been accepted, the organizer will usually send out a conformation letter complete with all the information that you need about the contest. You will be told when you can arrive, the size of your site, whether water and electricity are available, turn in times and anything else you need to make your final preparations.

Plan to arrive at the contest site as early as you can on the first day. It is a little easier to get into your site and set up if you arrive before many of the other teams. Introduce yourself to the contest Reps and let them know this is your first event. They will be sure to answer any questions that you may have. Set your site up, then relax a bit.

Be sure to keep meats cold before they are cooked. It is also a good idea to keep poultry separate from other meats. Please, don't keep the chicken with the beer either. Most organizers will provide in the contest packets what is expected of each team with respect to cleanliness and food safety. Be sure to follow these procedures to prevent food contamination. Remember, you are preparing food that will be eaten; you do not want any sick judges. When you arrive at the contest site, an official will inspect your meat before you can begin any rubbing or marinating.

After your meat is inspected, you can start your trimming and seasoning. Refer to your notes from your test cooks. Take your time and record what seasonings are used and what time they were applied.

The cooks' meeting is usually held on Friday evening. Here you will hear any last minute information pertaining to the contest. Questions are answered and last minute instruction is given. The Reps should have with them the official clock that will be used during the turn-in phase on Saturday. It is a good idea to synchronize the clock that you will be using with the official clock at this time. Boxes used for contest turn-in are often distributed at this time as well.

Take a couple of minutes on Friday evening to go over the plans and procedures as best you can with the other members of your team. Check your notes. Make sure each person knows what is expected and how things will be done. As in any team event, it is ideal when the team functions as a unit, as one. Planning and communication are the key to beginning to work toward that goal.

Be sure everyone knows the turn-in times and you have a reliable timepiece. Have the person who is running the boxes time his or her walk to the judges' table. First, so they know for sure where it is located. Second, you can calculate the time needed in the walk into your turn-in schedule.

Go over your notes and discuss how each meat will be treated. How will each entry be cut, sauced, and finished? Will you be using a grill to finish? Who will be responsible for preparing the fire, when should it be lit? Discuss the timing of each category.

If large crowds are expected, is there an alternate route or will you need a blocker? That's someone to walk ahead of the runner to make sure he is not plowed into by some out-of-control drunk (aka another BBQ cook), or a mother pushing a stroller, or a mother pushing a drunk in a stroller, or a drunk pushing his mother, well, you get the picture. If so, be sure the task is discussed and assigned, in an effort to prevent all of your hard work from ending up on the dirt path in the contest grounds. Not good.

I feel the most important piece of advice I can offer here is "pay attention to detail." I cannot stress enough the importance of preparation at this time. You will have a two-hour period during which each entry has 10 minutes to be submitted. The more confusion that you can reduce and or eliminate, the smoother things will run. You will have enough to deal with concerning getting the meats to the judges. You don't need additional distractions. Believe me, things will still go wrong that will have to be dealt with, that's what makes it exciting. After all, you still have Murphy's Law to overcome.

Just a few things to keep in mind while on site:

Be a good neighbor/competitor. Remember, we are all guests of the contest organizers, so treat the grounds as if they were your own. Put trash in the proper receptacle both in your site and after it's removed from your site. Keep your area neat.

Introduce yourself and your teammates to the folks around you. Strike up a conversation and get to know them. This is the easiest part of the whole contest, making new friends. If it looks like they need a hand with something, ask if you can help. They may return the favor before the weekend is over.

Stay in your assigned space. Most venues are fairly tight when it comes to site assignment. Use the space that is assigned to you, make sure that your team and guests do not encroach on your neighbor's site.

Do not become a part-time arborist. In other words, don't do any on-site pruning of the contest grounds trees and shrubs. Leave that work to the professions that have permission.

Bring firewood and marshmallow sticks from home.

Use alcohol in moderation. We make many jokes about drinking and drunken BBQ cooks here, all done in fun. The truth of the matter is most contest organizers ask that you be very discrete with your drinking, especially during the hours that the public is walking around. My thoughts on this matter are to be super discrete and not let it out of hand. We are guests in these venues and should not abuse the privilege, lest we are barred as a team or future contests are canceled completely, and nobody wants that. Use plastic cups and or can covers and make sure your teammates and guests don't get out of line. It's just good common sense. If someone in your crowd becomes a problem, deal with the matter before it becomes an issue and make sure it does not happen again. Make sure that you and your guests drink responsibly.

Remember to continue to care for your meats AFTER turn in time. If you have leftovers that are going home after the contest, be sure to cooler your meats as soon as possible after building your boxes. It does not take long for food to enter the "danger zone" after being cooked. Care must be taken here to prevent spoilage and ensure no one becomes ill from eating your food. Make sure to monitor and replenish the ice in your coolers as the addition of hot food items tends to melt the ice very quickly.

The awards ceremony is the most anticipated part of each contest. This is what everyone has come for. At the appointed time, you and the team should make your way to the area where the awards will be given. Here you will see all of the teams assembled as everyone anxiously await the announcer's voice. As the event proceeds, you will observe everyone offering their congratulations to those lucky enough to hear their name called. If your name is called, you then get to take what is known as "the walk" to the stage to accept your award.

This reminds me of what I read on one of the BBQ forums that I visit. It is hard to believe how much time and money a person will spend to win a $4.99 trophy with a plastic pig on it, words of wisdom there. I do not know how others feel, but for us, our plastic chicken and cow are priceless.

After the awards, the contest Rep will hand out the official scoring sheets to each team. Be sure to pick yours up. Here, you will see how each judge scored your entries and how you finished compared to the other teams. This sheet can be very helpful when it is time to evaluate the performance of the team.

While everyone's goal is to finish first and hear their team name called to the stage, remember this is your first contest, do not be discouraged. A realistic goal here would be to avoid the not so coveted DAL award. For which, you will not be called to the stage. In case you are wondering what the DAL award is, I will enlighten you. DAL means dead-ass last. Try to avoid this dubious distinction at all costs. But, that being said, should you happen to catch DAL in a category, don't sweat it. Once you have it out of the way, you have nowhere to go but up!

The contest is over, you and the team are all packed up and ready to head home. You are entering what I call "the danger zone." Let's be honest. No one has gotten the proper amount of rest and you have loss count of how many beers were consumed, not to mention the other forms of liquid refreshments that were available. You need to act responsibly here as well. Be sure that all of the drivers are rested and have NOT been drinking throughout the day. If your drive home is a long one, consider spending the night. Some contest venues will allow contestants to stay an additional night. If not, consider taking a motel room. The added expense is minimal compared to having someone fall asleep at the wheel or get a ticket for DWI. Again, common sense, use your head. Keep you and your teammates out of "the danger zone." Have a designated driver and use him. Or stay put until you are able to drive home safely.

# Chapter 20

## The Beltway BBQ Showdown 5/18-5/19 2007—Our First Contest

The date for our first contest was fast approaching and before I knew it, there it was. I ordered the meat, went over the trailer a dozen times checking and rechecking to make sure we would have everything we would need. This was the first year for this contest and I was not sure how many other teams would be attending. I knew of at least two other contests, one in Pennsylvania and the other in Virginia, scheduled for the same weekend. This would surely split up the teams that would be available to cook this weekend.

When we arrived we were met by the KCBS contest rep John Busch. I told him this was our first contest and he said if there was anything we needed, just let him know. He made us feel very welcome, explained the meat inspection and stopped by several times to make sure things were OK.

Once we had our meat inspected, we started the prep work. I had made some notes of how we wanted to season our different meats and with a good team effort, got our meat trimmed, rubbed and into the cooler ready to go into the smoker. We had one packer brisket, one brisket flat, 2 pork butts, 25 pieces of chicken and 4 racks of spare ribs.

It was not long and it was time to fire up the Caldera Tall Boy and get it up to temperature. We loaded the firebox with charcoal and lit it off. The big meats, (pork and brisket) go on first, and then you have a couple of hours to get a little shuteye before the ribs go in.

While sitting around having our morning coffee I thought it would be a good time to have a team meeting. I went over the duties and tasks that were ahead and outlined how I thought that they should be handled. I also went over our team expectations. I just wanted everyone to know no matter how we did, that we should not be disappointed if we did not get a call to the stage, this was our first contest after all.

We had been on time with all of our submissions and with the exception of just a few glitches, things went off very well. We talked about our turn-ins as we broke down the site, packed up the trailer and awaited the awards set for 4:00.

With only sixteen teams in the contest, the organizers decided to call the top five in each category. As we walked to the awards area, I again told the guys that they had done a great job and not to be discouraged if we did not hear our team name called. The awards are in the same order as turn-ins starting with chicken. The award for second place chicken goes to "who are those guys?" You could have knocked me over with a feather, unbelievable, I was floored, I think we all were. A call for chicken in our first contest, we were on cloud nine. I walked up to receive the trophy and floated back to the team as they stood clapping and beaming with smiles all around. Can you believe this? We were amazed.

We stood, clapped and congratulated the others on their calls and looked at each other in shock. Pork and ribs came and went without hearing our name again but it did not matter, we had a trophy for 2nd place chicken and that is all we needed. Brisket, the final category, and second place goes to "who are those guys?" Did he say us again? Flabbergasted was the only word that comes to mind. Two calls in our first contest, you would have thought we had just won a world championship.

As we walked back to the vehicles for the ride home, I think we were all in shock. We had finished 6th place in a 16 team field. When we split up, I thanked everyone for their efforts and promised to send the scoring breakdown that is given out after each contest by the judges. I would make copies and mail everyone their own.

We had worked very well together as a team, had a few laughs, ate some good food, met new friends, gotten two calls and just had a good time all around. We didn't know it for sure yet, but we were hooked.

# Chapter 21

### Box Building 101

I feel the first thing that I must do here is reiterate that I am not a competition expert, I have never won a Grand Championship in a contest. That being said, I do feel that I am able to comment on the basics for turn-in boxes for KCBS contests. I have done extensive research and continually strive to expand my knowledge on the topic. Building a decent box takes practice and patience. I again stress the importance of taking a class from a proven Champion and or hooking up with a team that has been on the circuit for a while to get some hands on training. Even after taking one or both of these suggested paths, you still should practice on your own before laying down cash money in the form of an entrance fee.

What I plan to do here is give you the basics of box building, as I know it. You can then take this information along with your other accumulated knowledge and move forward. I am not going to spend time here pretending that I can predict which way that the judges want to see each meat that you turn in. Whether you should slice, shred, or pull your pork. Chicken, breasts or thighs. These decisions should made by you and your teammates before it is time to make the box. I will explain what I feel constitutes a decent looking box and you can go from there.

For practice, get a stack of the containers used in a contest. The boxes themselves will be discussed later in this article. They are available at restaurant supply stores or you could ask your local carry out shop if they use a similar box and offer to buy a few from them. After assembling the box, they can be cleaned, washed and used again. After all, we are just practicing here.

When practicing, try different types of greens. See which ones you prefer to work with, what looks better with your product. What looks good to YOU. Go onto the Internet and look at boxes that others have prepared. See what methods they have used and what the end product looks like. Once you have an idea about how you want your box to look, you can move on to building the box.

Before you construct your first box, I think there are a couple of things that you should know. The total score given to each competitor consists of three categories, appearance, taste, and tenderness. Scores by each judge are given in whole numbers between 9 & 1. The scores for each category are weighted. Appearance scores are multiplied by 0.5714, thus making it the least weighted of the three. This fact does not diminish the importance of constructing the best box possible. In effect, appearance is not quite 1/3 of your score, but it is very important. My thinking here is, you may not be able to cook as good as the next guy, but there is absolutely no reason why your box can't be as good or better than his. With almost a third of the points up for grabs here, let's work to get the best-looking box that we can. I don't think it's that hard with a few basics in mind.

Appearance is the first of three criteria used by the judges to evaluate your turn-in. The Table Captain opens the box, then, presents it to the table of six judges that will evaluate your product. The Captain will hold the box open, walk it along in front of the judges, and allow all six to take a look. The judges will then mark their cards with the score for appearance. This is done before anything is removed from the box to be tasted. Once each judge records the appearance score, the next step begins. The judge cannot go back and change a score once recorded.

## KCBS Rule:

*Each judge will first score all the samples for appearance of the meat. The turn-in containers will then be passed around the table and each judge will place a sample from each of the containers in the appropriate box on the judging mat.*

The contest organizer provides the container. It is approximately 9"x 9" in size and is made of styrofoam. It is hinged in the back and has a self clipping fastener in the front. Be sure to identify the top and bottom before you do anything. The boxes are given out at the cooks' meeting. There is a number attached to the box. A number should be on each box that has been provided for each category that you will enter. The number should be the same for each of your boxes. Do not remove this number or let it become lost. The judges will need it to identify the box you hand in as yours. That is, of course, providing you WANT the judges to know what box is yours!

## KCBS Rule:

*Entries will be submitted in an approved KCBS numbered container, provided by the contest organizer. The number must be on top of the container at turn-in. The container shall not be marked in anyway so as to make the container unique or identifiable. Aluminum foil, toothpicks, skewers, foreign material, and/or stuffing is prohibited in the container. (Marked entries will receive a one (1) in all criteria from all Judges).*

Box building begins before you even arrive at the contest site. You must decide if you will use a garnish in your box and if so, which will it be. Your choices for garnish are limited by KCBS rules.

## KCBS Rule:

*Garnish is optional. If used, it is limited to chopped, sliced, shredded or whole leaves of fresh green lettuce, curly parsley, flat leaf parsley and/or cilantro. Kale, endive, red tipped lettuce, lettuce cores and other vegetation are prohibited. (Improper garnish shall receive a score of one (1) on Appearance).*

If you are going to use a garnish, it's a good idea to pick it up before you arrive at the contest venue. While shopping for your garnish, try and pick the best looking you can find. Don't be afraid to ask the produce man to take a look in the back to see if there is anything fresher available. I would suggest getting a little more than you think you will need in the event that some is lost or damaged before it is used.

Once you leave the store, care must be taken in the transportation of the material. If it is hot, a cooler is a good idea to have on hand already loaded with ice. Nothing wilts greens faster than hot humid summer air. After the greens are placed into the cooler, be sure to check on them from time to time. To make sure you have enough ice, and also to make sure they are not drowning in ice water.

Keep a check on the material throughout the weekend to be sure when you go into the cooler to use the garnish that it looks similar to the product you picked up in the store.

It is my personal opinion that garnish improves the look of the box, but again, it is optional.

While the use of garnish is sometimes a hot topic among BBQ cooks, one thing that most will agree on, if you are going to use garnish, it is a good idea to prepare your boxes ahead of time. Start early enough that you can take your time and do a thorough job. Wash the greens first. Then be sure to dry them so you do not get a build up of water inside the box. Separate the greens so you can see what you have to work with.

As you begin to place the greens in the box try and visualize what the box will look like when the meat is added. Remember, the garnish is meant to accent your turn-in product. Do not let the greens over power the box. In other words, don't over do it. Another thing to keep in mind at this time is balance. Try and balance the look of the garnish from top to bottom, side to side. Work to get all of the edges looking similar so that the eye is not pulled to one edge or the other. Think of it as a framing of your product.

Once you have the garnish in place, spread a wet paper towel over the greens, close the lid and place the box gently back into the cooler until needed. Again, make sure to stay away from any standing ice water in the bottom of the cooler. Prepare all of the boxes that you will need. Any unused greens should be placed into their original wrappings then returned to the cooler. Do not throw them away.

Now that you have the boxes ready to go, you can sit back and relax…. yeah right!

A few more things to keep in mind before you actually start to place your goods into the boxes

## KCBS Rule:

*Meat shall not be sculptured, branded or presented in a way to make it identifiable. Rosettes of meat slices are not allowed. (Violations of this rule will be scored a one (1) on all criteria by all six judges.)*

*Sauce is optional. If used, it shall be applied directly to the meat and not be pooled or puddled in the container. No side sauce containers will be permitted in the turn-in container. Chunky sauce will be allowed. Chunks are to be no larger than a fine dice. Sauce violations shall receive a score of one (1) on Appearance.*

To sauce or not to sauce. This is another hot topic of discussion. It is a decision that should be made well in advance of turn-in morning. If you decide to sauce, make sure that you do not overdo it and create puddling or pooling. Both of which will get you a score of one. Here, number one is not good.

Be sure to stay away from any presentation or preparation of your product that could be construed as marking, as mentioned above. Use common sense and keep in mind what the boxes look like that you have examined on the Internet. Again, it is not a good idea to try something that is experimental at your first contest.

One of the most important items that I will stress here is to be sure that you have met the criteria for serving portions for the product that you are going to put into your box. Below is the wording from the KCBS judges manual.

*Each contestant must submit at least six (6) separated and identifiable (visible) portions of meat in a container. Chicken, pork and brisket may be submitted chopped, pulled, sliced, or diced as the cook sees fit, as long as there is enough for six (6) judges. Ribs shall be turned in bone-in. Judges may not cut, slice, or shake apart to separate pieces. If there is not enough meat for each judge to sample, the shorted judge(s) will score a one (1) on all criteria, and the judges having samples will change the Appearance score to one (1).*

The short explanation here is each judge must be able to remove enough for a sample from the box without struggling to separate individual pieces. If you turn in shredded, pulled or chopped, be sure you have enough for six people to get a sample. Again, this is simple, yet seems to occur somewhat frequently. Don't let it happen to you.

The first thing you must do is select what will be placed into the box. Look at the selection of meat you have cooked. Try and select the best looking pieces. Don't forget to taste them as well. Once you have determined what tastes and looks best, you can begin to think about getting the product into your box. If you haven't already, put on your latex gloves before handling the meat.

If you are doing chicken pieces, try and pick six similar in size if possible. For ribs, it is a good idea to select six ribs from the same rack. The same with slices of brisket or pork. Uniformity is what you should be after.

When the time comes in the contest to begin to load the boxes, you should already have an idea from your practice sessions of how you want the product to look. One slight variable here is the final size of the individual pieces to be placed into the box. This will be the most important factor when deciding how much to place into your box.

I like to have a clean area in which to arrange the items you are going to place. Look at each piece and arrange them, on the work surface, as you would place them into the box. Your box is still in the cooler and this way as you change and arrange the food you are not messing up your carefully placed garnish. Try to arrange the items to be balanced and pleasing to the eye. You do not want to draw attention to any one spot. Remember, this is the judges' first look at your entry. I think it is human nature whether a judge will admit it or not, if something looks "good," it has a much better chance of tasting good.

Once you have the items arranged on the work area as you would place them in your box, remove a box from the cooler and place it on a *clean* surface next to your work area. Open the lid away from you so that you know the top and bottom of the box. Carefully transfer the items from the work surface to the box, arranging them just as they were on the table.

Now that the items are loaded in the box they way you want them, stand back and look the entire scene over. You may need to cut a few small pieces of your left over garnish to use as fillers. Carefully fill in any area that may be distracting in order to achieve a more balanced look to the box.

Look at the product in the box, does it appear straight, level, orderly? These are all factors, that in my opinion, can be distracting to the judges. Sometimes you can use additional garnish inserted underneath a piece of meat in order to raise it up to make it level with the others. Remember, nothing but the product and the garnish can be in the box.

After everything is where you want it, it is time to concentrate on the appearance of the meat. Are there any fingerprints or smudges in the sauce? Look for garnish stuck to a piece of meat that may be out of place. Does your product look moist enough? Will the judges be anxious to grab a piece?

Use a small sauce brush to take out any blemishes in the sauce that resulted from the movement into the box. Just be sure that you do not leave brush marks or even worse, bristles behind. If your meat looks dry, use a brush of thinned out sauce or a sprits of apple juice.

Once you are completely satisfied with the look of the meat, move you eyes outward and examine the garnish. Look again for uniformity. Check to see if you have left any smudges of sauce on the leaves. Use a paper towel to dab off any sauce you might find where it does not belong. Look the sides and lid of the box over, checking for sauce spots.

Here it's a good idea to have a teammate or two take a look. What do they think? Do they see anything that needs attention? Maybe they will pick up a smudge that you missed, or a brush mark. The more eyes the better.

Now is a good time to take a photo of the box. Take more than one so you will have something you can use. Stand over the box and shoot down, getting as close as possible. These photos will be very helpful to you after the contest is over when you evaluate your overall performance. They are also helpful to determine if you would like to make changes.

If you are satisfied, and if there is time, close the lid and walk away for a minute. Check to make sure the garnish does not obstruct the closing of the box. Walk back and open the box for a fresh look. Once you are sure, close it up and head to the judges' table.

Be very careful during the transportation to the turn in table. If there are large crowds at the contest, you may want to have someone walk ahead of the person carrying the box to act as a blocker and assure that no one walks into your precious cargo. Precaution and planning cannot be stressed enough.

# Chapter 22

## BBQ Gremlins; fact or fiction

BBQ gremlins, do they exist? Many have pondered this age-old question ever since the Caveman first put fire to meat. The debate has raged for years, rivaling the argument about Big Foot or the Loch Ness Monster. While I cannot say that I have ever personally observed these pesky creatures, I have observed the signs left behind when they decide to pay you a visit. I cannot say for sure, but if you ever get a chance to capture or possibly photograph one of these little buggers, you would be set for life. I will caution you however, that there are several alleged gremlin photos circulating around the Internet and in the supermarket tabloids, most have found to be fake.

Use caution if you see one, my advice would be to observe from a distance, take a photograph, then grab him by the throat and throttle the life out of him. (I realize that this sounds a bit harsh, but if they ever pay you a visit, you will know what I mean) You can then stick the remains in a bottle of formaldehyde and go on the carnival/daytime talk show circuit; you'll never have to work again, particularly after you appear on the Oprah Show.

The Salisbury Maryland Pork in the Park contest was scheduled for April 18th and 19th 2008. The weatherman promised good weather and then he delivered. Two days of sunny mild weather was just great for mid April in the Del Mar Va area. Contest organizer Sandy Fulton told me early on that

she had a weather connection. The first two years of this contest had rain for both days. It seems after a rocky start; Sandy has managed wonderful weather for this contest, I think she does have a weather guy! What gremlins?

Our team was really looking forward to our season opener and a chance to get everyone together again. The contest at Salisbury has really grown: in 2008 there were 83 teams. Some of the big names in BBQ were there which prompted many on the BBQ bulletin boards to say they would have to bring their A game, which I pretty much think they would have brought anyway. Did I hear a giggling gremlin?

Note to self: when cooking in a contest of many teams, do not wait until arriving in the town where the contest is to be held before buying your garnish. We stopped at a Food Lion as soon as we hit Salisbury. The green leaf lettuce had already been picked over, what was left was not very attractive. The produce manager said he would get another shipment in around noon on Saturday, that wouldn't do us much good unless we wanted to make a salad to eat on the way home. Not to worry, we bought four crappy looking bunches, (just in case), and we would run out later and grab a few, better looking heads. We did run out, we went to several stores and could not find a bunch of green leaf lettuce or parsley within 25 miles of the contest site, valuable lesson learned. The BBQ gremlins were just warming up.

We got set up without a hitch, met our neighbors, had a few beers and got the two Friday night categories turned in without too much difficulty. Later on our big meats went into our preheated Tall Boy Caldera right on schedule. A couple of fine cigars and all was well in our little corner of the world. We even had time for a little visiting. A nearly full moon along with warm temps made for a very delightful night. Who is afraid of a few gremlins?

Saturday morning at 5:30am, my alarm sounded. It was sometime around 6:00 when I drug my large behind out of the rack to get the ribs into the smoke. While I was at it, I would check temperature on the big meats which had been cooking all night. To sum it up, they were not where they should have been, they were behind, way behind. This set the tone for the entire day. I tried everything I could but the large cuts were just standing still, the only thing getting done was a flat and a butt I had in the WSM, if all else failed, we would have something to turn in. As meats were wrapped and finished, I would move others around between cookers. It was a game of musical chairs and the clock was ticking toward chicken time. I think the gremlins had stayed up working while we rested, or so it seemed.

Did I mention the grease fire? Sometime after breakfast, as I was steadily jacking the temp up in the Tall Boy, the Guru alarm sounded for a heat spike. I opened the door and found a grease fire in the lower section of the unit. Nothing like the smell of burning grease emitting from a cooker filled with unwrapped meat that was to be used for a contest entry. That ought to give us a good flavor profile! We extinguished the fire, cooled the cooker and moved on, what else could we do? It was nearing 10:00am. The gremlins were laughing their gremlin butts off now.

I was behind on starting my chicken prep and rushing was not fun. I got everything ready and into the cooker for the first leg of the cook which by all previous time studies would take about 1.5 hours. The chicken came to temp in 1 hour, how could that happen? Those damn Gremlins. There is nothing like holding chicken for 30-40 minutes while all of the juice slowly leaves the meat right before your eyes, oh what a feeling! What's that over there under the table?

The pork eventually came off at temp and feeling done. The ribs were pretty much on schedule, but a slight miscalculation in time caused them to be a tad over-cooked, but not too bad. The brisket was another story. We eventually got it to temperature, but it sure didn't "feel" done. We pulled and tossed everything into the cooler to rest and await turn in time. The gremlins had to be holding their sides by this time.

I think I can offer a brief summary of our entries. Chicken, rubbery skin, moist inside, tender meat. A beautiful testament to my winters trials and tribulations, can we say time well spent, I think not, gremlins again. Ribs, a little over cooked, not very pleasing to the eye, flavorful and tender, a bit dry. Pork, one butt felt very good, the other butt was like pot roast, overall, I thought it was our best pork submission yet. The brisket, we cooked two packers and a flat. The first flat from a packer I cut into for a taste test actually looked like it emitted a cloud of dust. Did somebody say dry? A repeat occurred on the next flat. This left the flat we had cooked solo. At least the knife would cut it, but I don't think I would go so far as to use the word tender or moist. That had to be gremlins I heard earlier, somebody get a net.

We got everything into the boxes, and by the way, our Lettuce Man Erich did a yeoman's job making good looking boxes from some nasty look- ing lettuce. We were behind in time during the entire turn-in procedure. The ribs, I wanted to take out and rebuild the entire box, but we were down to two minutes to go, we had to close the lid and send them in. Caution: gremlins at work.

As I was slicing the remaining brisket into pieces for the team to take home, I had to stop several times as I was overheating the electric knife. Man, that's what I call a tender brisket, who wants some? Needless to say, I brought home a ton of brisket meat that week. Oh well, it does make good chili. Maybe I'll feed it to the gremlins!

We packed up the gear and shuffled over for the awards. This was our fifth contest and I honestly sat down and thought there is no way we are getting a call in the strong field that was there. I was almost right, we heard our named called for 4th place pork. Our first call ever for pork, in a field of 83, not too bad. Just when we thought we ran the gremlins out of town, we left the contest without taking a team picture. I guess they got the last laugh.

While no official confirmed gremlin sightings were recorded in Salisbury that weekend we feel certain they were present. The signs they leave behind were everywhere at our site. I would swear to you that I could hear them laughing at me several times, especially right after I put out the grease fire, although, the laughter could have been coming from the teams around us but I really don't think that was likely. So, the myth continues. I cannot offer any solid evidence as to their existence, it is all circumstantial, as is evident by this story. I can only hope that their visits are not frequent, and hope not to see or hear them again for the rest of the season, and if I do, I think I have a trap that will work.

We had a ball, the weather was great. We saw some old friends and made some new ones, overall, the trip was a success. The score sheets would show we finished 16th overall, a decent effort in a very strong field. Not bad despite the best efforts of the BBQ Gremlins. As to their existence, I for one am a believer!

CHIX, SWINE & BOVINE Bbq.
*Because Bad BBQ is Downright Criminal.*

# Chapter 23

## Food Safety

Some food safety items are common sense. Some are required by KCBS rules. I would again suggest familiarizing yourself with the KCBS contest rules that outline specific steps that must be followed with regard to food safety. The KCBS rules can be found on their web site and most times are supplied by the contest organizer.

As I stated earlier, you must have you meat inspected by a contest official after you arrive at the contest site before you begin to inject, rub, season, or sauce. Meats can be trimmed ahead of time. Seasoning or injecting before the inspection is not allowed.

Your contest meats should be held in a cooler packed in ice at a temperature of 40 degrees or less. It is suggested that chicken be stored separately from other meats, but this is not required.

Smoking or the use of any tobacco products is not permissible while handling your meat products.

Hand washing—his should be understood. Wash your hands and remember what your mother said. We keep a 10-gallon Igloo cooler loaded all weekend with hot water. We use a large soup pot and a turkey fryer burner to heat the water then move it into the Igloo. It stays good and hot. The hot water can be used to wash your hands and for cleanup. There are several models of propane hot water heaters on the market and I understand that some are very efficient. No matter how you heat your water, remember to use it to wash your hands. It is the best defense you have against spreading germs and cross contamination.

Disposable latex gloves are suggested for use when handling the meat products, but again, are not required. If you use them, be sure to change often.

Use paper towels instead of cloth. My suggestion then would be to over-buy on paper towels. Have a roll or two accessible at all times in your cook area. Cloth dishrags and drying towels are a great place for bacteria to hide. Paper can be used, then thrown away, making for easier clean up and a more sanitary work area.

Bag and remove the trash from your site often, especially after food prep. Meat scraps, wrappers, blood-soaked paper towels and hot summer temperatures do not go well together.

Personal cleanliness of the all of the cooks, grills, smokers and cooking space is required. Per KCBS rules, food handlers are required to wear shirts and shoes at all times. Judging by the looks of some BBQ cooks including yours truly, the shirt rule is a blessing! As far as the shoe requirement, it must be a safety issue.

A three-tub washing station is required to be present at all contest sites. One tub of clear water, one for soapy water, and the last for sanitizing, (containing 1 cap of bleach per one gallon of water).

Be careful not to cross contaminate during the trimming and preparation process. When you finish prepping one item, wash all contaminated knifes, cutting boards, injectors etc. Spray the work surface with a cleaner that contains bleach. Wipe the work surface with a clean towel. Change your gloves before moving onto the next meat item. It is a good idea to get out the seasonings you will need prepping the meat you are working on before you glove up and handle raw meat.

A suggestion would be to have a teammate assist you. They would keep their hands clean and not handle the raw meat. When seasonings are needed, the clean and dry hands of the assistant would be used to dispense the product onto the meat, while your gloved and contaminated hands would be used to rub in the spice and turn the meat. A real team effort.

Rinsing or washing of your raw meat is not required by contest rules. I think it is a good step to add, as I always wash my meat in the home kitchen. Some cooks advocate the use of water mixed with a bit of vinegar as a bath for raw meat. I just use clean water.

After the meat has been cooked it must be held at 140 degrees or higher. If the meat is not to be held, it must be cooled within 2 hours to 70 degrees and within 4 hours to 41 degrees or less. Meat that has been cooled properly and then later reheated should be reheated to an all around temperature of 165 degrees for a minimum of 15 seconds before being served.

Make sure everything is washed clean before being stored away. If your next contest is in three weeks, you don't want to open a box and find your sauce brush becoming some type of scientific experiment.

Upon returning home be sure to chill and refrigerate any half used bottles of sauce, juice or any other perishable items. Things can get very warm stored away during hot summer months and care should be taken to prevent these items from spoiling.

When it comes to food safety, you can never be too informed.

# Chapter 24

## Afterwards

The first thing you will want to do upon arriving back home is to catch up on your rest. The last thing you will want to do is eat BBQ. Most say they want "anything but" BBQ to eat for a day or two after a competition. Many lively discussions have been held about what is the preferred food to eat after a competition. This is a personal decision. My preference is pizza.

Once you have caught up on your rest—preferably the next day—go over your contest notes. Make a note if there is anything you can remember that you would like to change. Note what went well, what did not. Believe me; this is best as soon as possible after the contest. Once you immerse back into your regular everyday grind, the small details seem to run away. The small details are what we are after. Remember, pay attention to detail.

Go over your notes from the contest cook. Compare to the notes from your test cooks. Does something change? Was the outcome better? Add notes as necessary if there was something that worked, or didn't. This is the best time to review.

Review the cook with your teammates. What did they think, any suggestions for improvements, changes? Maybe they saw something you missed, or offer a change to improve. In my opinion, the collective thoughts of the team are better than the solitary thoughts of the Big Cheese, even if you don't let on that they helped!

Review your supply list. Are there any supplies that need to be restocked? Be sure to grab them before the next contest. This is the purpose of keeping a list.

Also, review your equipment list. Did you have everything you needed? If you hauled it, did you use it? Is there anything that would make the contest more enjoyable or easier next time? Be sure to make a note now, not later.

Go over your score sheet. Break it down as best you can. Try to determine where you need improvement. Remember, appearance, taste, and tenderness. Where were you strong? Where do you need work? These sheets can be very helpful in the evaluation of your performance. I make copies, mail them to all of the team members so they can have a look, and help analyze.

I like to visit the bulletin boards and forums after a contest and see what others have to say. What did others think about the contest overall, the judging, their own performance? Some teams will post photos of their turn-in boxes, go onto their web-sites and take a look. How did they compare to yours? You may even consider posting pictures of your own boxes to get input from others. Be sure to offer congrats to the folks that were called to the stage. It is the neighborly thing to do.

After things return to normal and you get the smoke out of your clothes, it is time to look ahead to the next contest. If there is time, continue to work with your test cooking. The more you can do, the better off you will be in the end. The worst thing you can do is unload your truck and not use your smoker for a month until you get it out to load for the next event. Just like any other sport or pursuit, practice, practice, practice. If you want to improve, you have got to practice.

**PORK & DEANS**

BBQ Team

# Chapter 25

### Too much of a good thing?

I can remember a time when just the smell of a SIA, (smoker in action), would set my mouth to watering. I remember when the first contest was held in my hometown of Bel Air, Maryland. I rode around the streets on Saturday morning just to whiff the air. That was the truth. Intoxicating would be putting it lightly. As the old saying goes, that was then, this is now.

One would think that if a fellow was into cooking BBQ contests, well, that guy must love his BBQ. I remembered a thought I had while driving home from the Bel BBQ Bash after first meeting my friend Steve Farin with several zip lock bag full of BBQ'd delights. Why in the world would a BBQ guy give away all of these fine eats? I just couldn't figure it out. It made no sense to me.

A subsequent conversation with Steve when I cooked with him at Salisbury helped fill in the blanks. "I just can't eat that stuff any more," Steve told me on Saturday after the turn ins, as I once again loaded up my zip locks with Steve's championship submissions. How could that be? I thought. Oh well, all the more for me, no sense in it going to waste.

The family would be waiting in the driveway upon my return if they knew I was in possession of bags of smoky goodness from Steve. As I arrived back at the homestead, there were no questions, how was the trip? Did you have fun? How did you do? The only question I would hear is "where is the cooler?" My, how times have changed.

After cooking a couple of hundred pounds of Que in the past 3 years I can honestly say, "I can't eat that stuff." Well, maybe not that direct, so let me explain. When we travel to a BBQ contest we always have a camp meal on Friday night, one thing is certain, it won't be BBQ. Pasta, seafood, steak, anything but BBQ.

Saturday during turn-ins we have to sample our product as we proceed through the schedule. I have to tell you, when we get to brisket, the last turn-in, I sometimes have trouble taking a sample. When the contest is over, and its time to divide the remains, I have to force myself to take some home. Even the other guys on the team have become less than excited when it comes to left-overs. When we first started this operation, there would sometimes be shoving matches while divvying up the take outs. Today, when asked who wants some Que to take home, sometimes, the only shoving is the team members knocking each other over to get away from the bagged goods. Amazing.

After a contest, I don't want any BBQ for at least a couple of days. Saturday dinner when I return from a contest weekend is usually pizza, fresh fish or a crab cake, anything but the 4 KCBS meats, and especially nothing that has been anywhere near a brush filled with BBQ sauce.

Much has been written and discussed on the various BBQ forums that I visit from time to time about what others prefer to eat after a contest weekend. Some prefer sweets, pasta is another favorite. There does seem to be a consensus among most BBQ cooks, ANYTHING BUT BBQ. While it is very hard to get two cooks to agree on anything, there does not seem to be much disagreement on this question.

Upon reflection, I gotta say I don't much like it. It almost seems that I have lost my desire for BBQ'd meats, I know my family has. I guess that they could be justified in their lack of desire for my Que. They have eaten an awful lot of BBQ product in the past 36 months. (I won't even mention the Chicken Obsession of 2008) They never request Que for dinner anymore, who could blame them. My biggest complaint is, I no longer want BBQ for dinner either, or for lunch for that matter.

This past holiday season I cooked several slabs of spares to take to a Christmas party. I ate one small rib to test for seasoning, that was it. At the party when they were served, I opted for a ham sandwich and a bowl of soup. Wow, I can hardly believe it myself.

I will still eat and sample my product as I test cook for the upcoming competition season, but to make a meal of "that" stuff, I think not. I think I'll just have a salad. On second thought, last weekend as I was working on my chicken attack, I stumbled upon a new twist for my formally feathered friend that has some possibilities. I made the same recipe again this weekend for a football party and actually found myself going back for seconds, hmm-mmm I could be onto something here.

Maybe, it's just like another old saying goes, too much of a good thing. Not that I am trying to say my product is good, well, you get the point, maybe it's just too much Que. I sure hope not. I know that through the power of positive thinking and a lot of hard work, I can recapture my desires of old and once again learn to "crave the Que." I can't wait!

# Chapter 26

**To shig or not to shig.......that is the question**

My first experience with shigging was during my time spent cooking with my friend Steve Farin. I had no idea when I first met Steve that he was one of the top BBQ cooks on the East Coast or the country for that matter. What I can tell you is, during prep time, Steve has an awful lot of visitors, some are much more obvious with their shigging than others. When Steve moves from inside of his trailer to the back area near his cookers, it is like E.F. Hutton speaking, everyone within eyesight of the cooker door stops what they are doing in hopes of getting a look. I am exaggerating here, as I am sure you know, but the fact remains, it is very obvious when you see shiggers in action. Sometimes, it's not very pretty.

Shigging in some form or another exists in all sports. Scouting the opponent has become acceptable in most of the stick and ball sports today. All professional teams make extensive use of game films in their regular preparation for each game. Although, filming an opponent in what is supposed to be a "private" practice session is considered a no-no, just ask Bill Belichick.

In addition to making use of film and scouts, many pro teams have people on staff who attempt to intercept the opposing teams signals. Some even employ lip readers, as is evident each Sunday when the close ups of the coaches show words being spoken behind folders and sheaves of paper. Who does not remember playing little league baseball trying to figure out if the other team was going to bunt?

Why should it be any different in competition BBQ? Some would say it is not. Many competitors have very strong feelings about the topic, both pro and con. Still others, go to great lengths to prevent shigging, while some, have been known to go to extreme lengths just to shig. Let's take a look at both sides of the discussion.

First, let's have a look at the shigger. I think I must separate the degrees of shigging, lets call it intentional and unintentional. Contest sites, by their nature, are many times small and crammed together. Teams are set up in close proximity to each other. Sometimes, only a few feet separate your prep area to your neighbors. Shigging, to some degree, is almost unavoidable. Slow cooking large hunks of meat is not exactly an intensely active sport, leaving a lot of down time. If the team next door is doing something while you are idle, sometimes its only natural for your eyes to wander in that direction. This would have to fall into the category of unintentional shigging, done WITHOUT intent to steal methods or secrets. Intent being the key word here.

My advice in this situation is try not to gawk. If you are interested in what the neighbor is doing to his chicken, take a quick look then look away, sort of like looking at the sun, just don't stare. I have seen some guys take up an unobstructed position, get comfortable, and settle in, like they are at the movies, this, is not being a good neighbor. This would be called intentional shigging, in my opinion. No one likes being stared at, least of all while preparing an entry for a contest.

Another tip to be an indiscrete shigger is to involve some teammates. Make sure it is clear what you want to observe, then take turns glancing, meet up later to exchange notes. This method is a little less obvious and intrusive. The other option is just to go over and ask your neighbor what he is doing to his chicken. Most of the folks that I have run into around this game are very friendly and will tell you just about anything you ask them. This way, you lessen the risk of slicing a finger off while shigging your neighbor as you trim your brisket.

The next, and possibly the lowest form of shigger is the intentional, in-your-face shigger. This guy I can't explain. I have never had the experience of seeing one in action, I have heard several stories that I have a hard time believing. Although, sometimes I wonder how someone can toss litter out the window of a car, but let me tell you folks, they are out there. A competitor who has won more than his share of contests once told a group of cooks about a neighbor he had at a contest. The neighbor spent the entire weekend trying to get a look into the cooks' site. During turn-ins, the neighbor had erected a step ladder, in order to get a better view, while the successful cook was building his turn in boxes. If memory serves me correctly, the shigger was trying to take a picture of the box after it was built.

Another contestant related a tale on the Brethren Forum of a nearby cook walking into his prep area, picking up a rub container, dumping some of the contents into his hand, then walking away, never saying a word. These folks, my friends, aren't your typical competition cooks. Slug is a word that comes to mind; this is the same guy that WOULD toss a paper bag out the window of a car onto the street.

While I certainly do not have much experience being shigged, I will offer what I feel are several easy steps you can take to prevent shigging, or at the very least, could serve to help confuse the shigger. The first, and most obvious, is to erect a tent or screen for your area. This method seems to be gaining in popularity. There are some folks that have a real problem with teams erecting screens, to me, its no big deal. The only problem I see here is the chance you may offend your neighbor. This may or may not be of concern to you. Most teams would not care if you erect a screen, especially if they have been around a while. I think it might only offend a new team that had not been 'screened' before. Teams that use campers or enclosed trailers have built in screens and can choose to operate within the enclosure, thus ensuring all the privacy needed. This is the ultimate in anti-shigging.

Some other, more subtle ways to prevent wandering eyes can be done when setting up your area. Using your own equipment as blockers is a common method. Choosing the back, or less populated side when picking a spot for your main workspace is another easy fix. Also, the use of team banners to obstruct the view of any would be shiggers is a widely accepted, less obvious practice.

Other, more time consuming methods are employed by some on the circuit. The transfer of sauces and rubs into unmarked or miss marked containers is one of the more popular methods. This would not work for me. I have trouble remembering what day it is, trying to remember what rub is in the wrong container, well, it just wouldn't work.

There is also the deception method. Getting your brisket out of the cooler, laying it up on the table, gloving up, then rubbing the brisket for 5 or 10 minutes before returning it to the cooler is sure to cause a stir to anyone that is intent on watching your every move. Lets don't forget the fake application method. This requires a bit of separation between shigger and shiggee. Using a closed container, such as cayenne pepper, "hey Al, hand me the red pepper," said in somewhat of a loud voice, is the first part of the deception. Take the container, without opening it, then applying very liberally to any exposed meat can cause a group of unsuspecting shiggers to really scratch their heads. All in good fun of course. The trick here is to be sure that you do not open the container before attempting to deceive the nearby shigger.

The most pressing question I have to ask: is there a benefit or detriment to shigging? I feel the answer has to be, no to benefit, yes to detriment. Let me explain, in response to a post that I made on the Brethren Forum, http://www.bbq-brethren.com/forum/, a reply that was posted made a lot of sense to me. You could give 10 people the same cake mix, ingredients and equipment, and the end result would be 10 different cakes. Some would be great, others not fit for doorstops. This thought process can be taken to the next level, competition BBQ classes. Many of the top flight BBQ teams give classes all around the Country. The difference between this and shigging is you are INVITED to watch at the classes and take notes. The other small difference is, you are usually writing a large check before getting into the class.

Nevertheless, my point is, if everyone could do what the Championship Teams are doing that are giving the classes, logic would say that each team that takes a class, would automatically become a champion. I don't think this is the case. So, is there any benefit in wasting time and energy trying to see who is doing what to their chicken, my answer would be no.

My personal comment on the matter is, who has time to shigg? When I am at a contest, especially on Saturday morning, I hardly have enough time to take care of everything I need to, without worrying about what the guys next to me are doing. By the time I can slow down enough to take a look around, the only thing I might be able to learn is how the neighbor is scrubbing his grates or putting out his fire, guarded secrets, these are not.

Is there a detriment in being labeled as a "big time shigger?" Well, if that sort of thing bothers you, then the answer is yes. At the very least, obvious shigging, in my opinion, is rude and unacceptable in the contest setting. I will, however, toss in this one little caveat. Subtle shigging can be some harmless fun, especially when you throw in team participation, accompanied by some trash talking and good natured ribbing along with a few cold beers, and now you've got some good solid laughs. For the most part, teams are playing this game to have some fun. Keep it friendly.

As for now, we don't have any real problem with shiggers. To be blunt, nobody really cares what we are doing when we are at a contest. We could set our prep table up out on the midway and would not draw a crowd, unless it was a hungry contest watcher looking for a hand out, or directions to the men's room. I guess that is how you know when you've 'arrived" on the BBQ circuit, when you are shigged. Let's just say that Who Are Those Guys? will not be erecting screens any time soon.

I think the most important lesson here is to try to be a good neighbor. Always respect your neighbor's privacy, even if it means staring at the blank side of a screen on Saturday. If you want to know what he is doing, why not just ask him. Judging by the many nice folks that I have met during our short time on the competition circuit, I'll bet he'll answer your question and then some. Who knows, you might get lucky and find that you've made a good friend for life, which in my opinion, is much more valuable than any BBQ secret!

# Chapter 27

### A Playlist—Contest Tunes

One of the most important aspects of any cooking or entertainment operation is the background music. Think about it, have you ever been to a party where there was no music? How about where the music selection was made by a head banger teenager or worse yet, where they have the radio playing? Face it, good tunes, good food, and good fun go together like Larry, Moe and Curley, there is no better combination. Of course, I am speaking of the 3 original Stooges, again, there were no better.

Over the years, I have come to appreciate many different styles and types of music. I have also become a collector of music related to BBQ. My family gave me an iPod several years ago for Christmas and since then I have been off and running. I have a huge selection of tunes on board and never leave home without my iPod, the player, and several additional hookup cables in case an emergency arises. I have BBQ tunes, blues, classic rock, oldies, western swing, barbershop, hip hop and everything in between. Many times, I think folks invite me to parties just to hear my music and could care less if I even show up. Usually the first question I am asked upon arriving at the party is, "Did you bring your iPod?"

I believe the same thinking applies to the contest setting. A decent collection of background music, played at an acceptable level, helps establish that all important "mojo" that a team needs to complete its tasks in a timely manner. It also helps accomplish the most important contest goal, and that is to have fun. The important phrase here is "played at an acceptable level." Remember, the teams next to you may be playing their own music and may not want to hear some head banging music played at high volume. Again, use common sense and be considerate. Also, remember to observe contest 'quiet times' when asked to do so.

Years of searching the forums, web sites, and Internet music sources have helped me assemble a decent collection of BBQ related tunes. Some are very popular and widely available, others more obscure and harder to find. I have broken the songs down into a play list of sorts to be used on turn-in morning. My ultimate goal was to construct a list that I could start at 10:00 on Saturday morning and let play through the morning until cleanup was complete. The songs would be played in such a way that I would know what time it was just by hearing the song. I haven't quite had time to refine the list to that point, but feel I have assembled a good list with some decent tunes, so what if I still have to look at the clock?

You can see by reading the list I have included an assortment of non-BBQ tunes to help balance the selections. Although the theme and message still applies and is consistent in most cases. Time, heat, pressure, drinking, fire or smoke are present in most titles and provide a decent mix to the BBQ selections. Use it as a guideline or in its entirety, whatever it takes to get your contest mojo workin'.

**Prep time:**
*Bang on the Drum All Day* (Tod Rundgren)
*Pressure* (Billy Joel)
*Please throw this bone dog a bone* (Junior Wells)
*Hotter than a Two dollar Pistol* (George Jones)
*Take this job and shove it* (Johnny Paycheck)
*Kidney Stew Blues* (Eddie 'Cleanhead' Vinson)
*No No Song* (Ringo Starr)
*I Gotta get Drunk* (Willie Nelson)
*Bubbles in my Beer* (Bob Wills)
*Chug-A-Lug* (Roger Miller)
*Whiskey Bent & Hell Bound* (Hank Williams, Jr.)
*Cocktails for Two* (Spike Jones)
*Cigarettes, Whiskey and Wild Woman* (Tex Ritter)
*Working in a Coal Mine* (Sam Cooke)
*Time in a bottle* (Jim Croce)
*Time is Tight* (Booker T and the MGs)
*Blowing the Fuses* (Brownie McGee)
*As time goes by* (Louis Armstrong)
*Wango Tango* (Ted Nugent)
*Bless this Barbeque* (Billy O'Rourke)
*I'm in a Hurry to get things done* (Alabama)

**Chicken:**
*Drink that Mash and Talk That Trash* (Flat & Scruggs)
*A Chicken Aint Nothin But a Bird* (Nellie Lutcher)
*Chicken Shack Boogie* (Bootleg Kings)
*Chicken Stuff* (Hop Wilson)
*The Chicken Song* (Ernest Tubb & Red Foley)
*Tennessee Bird Walk* (Jack Blanchard)
*Surfin Bird* (The Trashmen)
    (not a chicken tune, but who can argue 'the bird is the word')
*Barnyard Boogie* (Louie Jordan)
*Gotta Sell Them Chickens* (Hank Thompson)
*Barnyard Banjo Picken* (Stringbean)
*Dixie Chicken* (Little Feat)
*Aint Nobody Here But us Chickens* (Louie Jordan)

*Little Red Rooster* (Howlin Wolf)
*Sic em on a Chicken* (Zac Brown Band)
*Time is on my Side* (Rolling Stones)

## Ribs:
*Under pressure* (David Bowie & Queen)
*Barbecue Shoes* (Blue House)
*Salt Pork West Virginia* (Louie Jordan)
*Smoke gets in your eyes* (The Platters)
*Barbeque* (Robert Earl Keen)
*Tube Steak Boogie* (ZZ Top)
*Good BBQ* (The Riptones)
*19th Nervous Breakdown* (Rolling Stones)
*Leons BBQ* (Dave Nevling)
*Another One Bites the Dust* (Queen)
*Bad to the Bone* (George Thorogood)
*Badly Bent* (The Tractors)
*BBQ Stain* (Tim McGraw)
*Got my Mojo Workin* (Muddy Waters)

## Pork:
*Put Another Log on the Fire* (Tom T Hall)
*Ring of Fire* (Johnny Cash)
*Barbeque* (Robert Earl Keen)
*Ain't goin' Down till the Sun Comes Up* (Garth Brooks)
*Beans & Cornbread* (Louie Jordan)
*I Love My Babys BBQ* (RJ's Rhythm Rockers)
*Dizzy Miss Lizzy* (The Beatles)
*Whos gonna feed them hogs?* (Tom T Hall)
*The Barbeque Song* (Rhett & Link & The Homestead Pickers)
*Fire Down Below* (Bob Seagar)
*Rock & Roll Part 2* (Gary Glitter)
*Middle of the Road* (The Pretenders)
*For Those About To Rock* (ACDC)
*Barbecue* (Washboard Sam)
*A little less conversation* (Elvis Presley)

## Brisket:
*Taking Care of Business* (BTO)
*Big Balls in Cowtown* (Asleep at the Wheel)
*Feed my Frankenstein* (Alice Cooper)
*Got me under pressure* (ZZ Top)
*Beast of Burden* (Rolling Stones)
*As good as I once was* (Toby Keith)

*Fire* (Arthur Brown)
*Rawhide* (Blues Brothers)
*Milk Cow Blues* (Bob Wills)
*Mess Around* (Ray Charles)
*Cut the Mustard* (Bobby Bare)
*Cheeseburger in Paradise* (Jimmy Buffet)
*Cattle Call* (Roy Rogers)
*At Last* (Etta James)

## Cleanup:
*Too Much Barbecue* (Big Twist and the Mellow Fellows)
*They don't serve BBQ in Hell* (Cary Swinney)
*Too Hot to Trot* (The Commodores)
*All my Rowdy Friends* (Hank Williams, Jr.)
*Barbeque* (Hayseed Dixie)
*A Little Help from my Friends* (The Beatles)
*Barbeque* (Ray Stevens)
*Pappas got a brand new bag* (James Brown)
*Paying the Cost to be the Boss* (BB King)
*Sheriff's Barbecue* (Clarence 'Gatemouth' Brown)
*See You Later Alligator* (Bill Haley)
*She's Gone Gone Gone* (J D Crowe and the New South)
*Celebration* (Kool and the Gang)

A Truce in the Feud to Bring you the Que

# Chapter 28

### Final thoughts

I hope I have given you some insight as to what would be involved in the creation of your own competition BBQ team. I have tried to cover the many issues that may arise along the way, at times, offering my opinion. Many of my suggestions are based on my own experiences. Some are as a result of my years of research on the topic. My methods, theories, and opinions are not meant as absolutes, but are offered to help guide you through the process and hopefully make it a little easier. Take what you can from here, add it to your own research and jump on in, you will enjoy the ride.

One thing that I can guarantee, you will not find anywhere else, a group of competitors that shows more sportsmanship and willingness to help others than the folks involved in the competition BBQ circuit. While at a contest in Dover DE, a strong windstorm blew through the contest grounds about ten o'clock Friday night causing damage to equipment belonging to many teams. The most asked question I heard after the storm was, "Are you all right? Do you need anything?" Teams that had received minor damage were out helping those that were more severely affected. Equipment was repaired and lent to others without hesitation. I have observed this phenomenon many times, and will say that in today's world, it would be considered very unusual. There are a great bunch of folks involved in this sport, and I am proud to be a participant.

BBQ, it's not just competition, it's a lifestyle.

Hope to see you out there on the BBQ Circuit.

Think Smoke!!!

# Chapter 29

## Some Common Competition BBQ Terms

Words to que by….or….do you speak que?

I found over my years of reading BBQ bulletin boards and other various sources, just like any other sport, BBQers have their own phraseology. Sometimes the definition is obvious; sometimes it took a little digging around to come up with a meaning. This is by no means a complete list. It is as accurate as I can be. I think that by knowing a few of the words used, it may help you along in your journey down the BBQ trail.

### Anything butt
Sometimes called "chefs choice." This is a contest category in addition to the 4 KCBS entries, usually meaning anything other than the regular required meat products. It is a good idea to check with the individual contest organizer to get a specific explanation as to the rules and regulation pertaining to this event, as they are often times different than the standard. In a KCBS event, this category does not apply to the overall contest score.

### ABT
An acronym for "Atomic Buffalo Turd." Take a jalapeño pepper, slice in half, stuff with cream cheese and other chopped up goodies, insert into the smoker until soft. Or better yet, go onto the BBQ Forum and ask "what is an ABT?" Nah, on second thought, I really do not want to see you "flamed." The best thing to do would be to go to the Forum archives and search ABT and get a good recipe. Don't make the same mistake that I did.

### Barbecue, BBQ, Barbeque, Bar-b-que, Bar-B-Q, Bah B Que
As per *Wikipedia*: a method and apparatus for cooking food, often meat, with the heat and hot gases of a fire, smoking wood, or hot coals of charcoal and may include application of a marinade, spicerub, or basting sauce to the meat. The term as a noun can refer to foods cooby this method, to the cooker itself, or to a party that includes such food. The term is also used as averb for the act of cooking food in this manner. Barbecue is usually cooked in an outdoor environment heated by the smoke of wood or charcoal. This activity is often combined with the consumption of ice cold adult beverages.

## Beef Brisket

Taken from the front chest of a beef cow, a brisket has two parts, the flat and the point, also known as the deckle. The flat section is typically more lean than the fattier point cut. A layer of fat attaches these two sections. Together, both pieces are known as a packer brisket, (point & flat). Most teams submit the flat cut in their turn-in box. In competition, corned beef is not allowed. The brisket meat can be chopped, sliced, pulled or diced for turn in according to KCBS guidelines.

## Best Part

See "call" and "walk."

## Burnt Ends

Chopped meat that has been smoked or cooked for a long time creating a burnt-like crust, ideally moist on the inside. Often times made with the point of a beef brisket that has been separated from the flat, returned to the cooker for several hours, chopped, sauced then served. Sauce is a popular optional.

## CAB

Certified Angus Beef. A brand of beef that requires its suppliers to meet certain criteria for the beef that is sold under its name.

## Call

At the awards section of a BBQ contest when the announcer requests your presence on the stage to receive an award, this is known as "a call." Followed quickly by "the walk." (see Walk; also see Best Part)

## Ceramic Cookers

Big Green Egg, Komodo Kamado, Grill Dome, and Primo are some of the makers of these types of cookers. Ceramic cookers are made of various materials some of which may or may not contain ceramics. Materials include "space age" ceramics, terra cotta, refractory materials and portland cement mixed with lava rock. The walls of ceramic cookers walls are heavy and thick with the thickness varying depending on the maker. The temperature tolerated by these materials varies, but most makes can easily withstand cooking temperatures up to 1000 degrees. However, you should follow the instructions that come with your particular cooker. This cooker allows you to sear your steaks at 700 degrees or more, smoke your barbecue at 200 degrees or less, and roast and bake at all temperatures in between. Ceramic cookers will maintain the temperature you set due to their good insulating characteristics, and perform well at high and low temperature settings.

## Chefs Choice

See "anything butt."

## Chicken

Chicken includes Cornish Game Hen and Kosher Chicken. Whole chickens or pieces are acceptable. Chicken may be chopped, sliced, pulled or diced. If whole chicken is used it must be separated in such a way that each of the six judges can take a portion.

## Chief Cook

You can call it the boss of the sauce, head chef, dictator, pitmaster, chief cook, postmaster general, grand poobah, president, CEO, HMFIC, or just plain King. Someone has to be in charge, call the shots, and make the decisions. Every team needs someone to be the boss. To take credit when things go right, and to assign blame when they go wrong, just like at work. The only exception to this declaration is when the wife is on site, we all know who's the boss then, don't we?

## Clonesickle

Information obtained by a Google search finds that this term was started by Darren of the Smokin' Clones BBQ team. It is a bottle of Jack Daniels (or any other of your favorite elixir), frozen in a block of ice. The neck is kept above the level of the ice cube so that the contents of the bottle can be consumed. Beware; too much contact between the open neck and your mouth can result in unpredictable behavior, a bad headache, and/or a very rough following day.

## Completely confused

The term used to describe my brain after reading the definitions and explanations of the words marinate and marinade (see below); or my brain after contact with the open end of a clonesickle. (see above)

## DAL

Dead ass last—this is a finishing spot to be avoided at all costs. If you happen to find yourself in this position, the good news is you have nowhere to go but up!

# DQ
Disqualified/no score/removed from consideration/not good.

# Egger
A person that cooks on a Big Green Egg cooker. Also known as an egg-head.

# Fattie (phattie)
Not a nickname for your BBQ partner but a BBQ snack prepared with a roll of ground sausage, sometimes stuffed, rolled and coated with BBQ rub then smoked for an hour or so in the smoker until done. MmmmMm-mmgoood!

# Flamed
The response received from some persons posting on various BBQ boards when a newbie asks what some of the others consider to be a dumb question. Sometimes warranted, sometimes not.

# Garnish
Garnish is optional. If used, it is limited to chopped, sliced, shredded or whole leaves of fresh green lettuce, curly parsley, flat leaf parsley and or cilantro. Kale, endive, red tipped lettuce, lettuce cores and other vegetation are prohibited. Improper garnish shall receive a score of one on appearance.

# Grand Champion
In a KCBS contest, the highest scoring team, after combining the scores from the four main categories, (chicken, ribs, pork, and brisket), is known as the Grand Champion.

# IBCA
International Barbeque Cookers Association, a sanctioning body based in Arlington, Texas. www.ibcabbq.org

# KCBS
Kansas City Barbeque Society—based in Kansas City—Sanctioning body for BBQ contests. http://www.kcbs.us

# Marinade
(Noun) A liquid for which to soak your meat in prior to cooking. Marinading/marinaded are considered verbs defined as to marinate.

**Marinate**

(Verb) The process of soaking your meat in a liquid prior to cooking.

**Marination**

To become marinated.

**Minion Method**

An effective method for lighting charcoal in your cooker popularized by Jim Minion, hence the name, "The Minion Method." By using this method for starting your fire it is possible to help extend the burn time for your load of fuel for a longer period, of course, dependent on weather conditions. A short synopsis of the method follows. For a more detailed account, I suggest you Google the term and do some in depth research. The concept is a simple one, Place a small number of hot coals on top of a full load of unlit charcoal in the fuel chamber. Control the amount of air entering your cooker to keep the fire burning low and slow. The unlit fuel catches fire gradually throughout the cooking session, resulting in longer burn times.

**MIM-SCN**

Memphis in May Sanctioned Contest Network, sanctioning body based in Memphis, Tennessee. www.memphisinmay.org

**Mop sauce**

This is generally a thinned out liquid that is applied, sometimes with a mop like tool, to meats during the cooking process. The thinking is to add flavor and to keep the product moist.

**Newbie**

A person or a team just beginning in the competition BBQ circuit. Not a derogatory term, everyone has to start somewhere.

**Official Time**

Time kept by the contest official and used to determine when products can be submitted to the judges. Usually based on the atomic clock which transmits to most cell phones. (see also "turn-in time")

**Offset cooker**

Common type of BBQ cooker usually having a firebox at one end with an exhaust chamber at the other end. The cooker chamber located in the middle. Food is cooked by the heat and smoke being drawn from one end to the other at a constant temperature. Some are set up fairly simply, while other, more efficient models employ baffles and heat deflectors to regulate and even out the heat.

## Pellet Cooker

A cooker built with an electric feeding system used to deliver wood pellets similar to the ones used to heat some homes. The pellets are made specifically for cooking and are available in many flavors

## Pork Ribs

Ribs shall include the bone. Country style ribs are not allowed.

## Pork

Pork is defined as Boston Butt, Picnic and/or Whole Shoulder, weighing a minimum of five pounds. Pork shall be cooked (bone in or out) and shall not be parted. May be chopped, sliced, pulled or diced.

## Pork butt

A cut of pork located on the top front shoulder of the pig, above the picnic cut. Also referred to as the Boston butt. Not from the rear, that is known as the ham.

## Qualifier

When pertaining to BBQ contests indicates the Grand Champion of that event will have their team name placed into a pool for the draw to the Jack Daniels World Championship Invitational Barbecue contest held in October in Lynchburg, TN. They also are eligible to participate in the American Royal Invitational held in Kansas City.

## Reserve Champion

In a KCBS contest, the second place team, after combining the scores from the four main categories, (chicken, ribs, pork, and brisket), is known as the Reserve Champion

## Rub

A mixture of seasonings, wet or dry, applied to your meat products before cooking.

**Rub your meat**

Term used to describe the application of seasonings to various BBQ meats, usually done before the meat is inserted into the cooker. Nothing more.

**Sanctioned Event**

Events that are sanctioned by a recognized BBQ society and or association. The event is usually operating within the rules and guidelines for that particular organization.

**Sauce**

Most times applied towards the end of the cooking process. The use of which is optional in KCBS contests. If used, be sure not to apply too much as to create puddles or pools which would be grounds for disqualification.

**Sauced**

A common term used to describe ones condition after becoming too familiar with the business end of a clonesickle. (see definition for clonesickle above). Can also be used to describe your meat after you have coated it with any type of sauce.

**Shigging**

Verb 1) Entering another teams site with intent of stealing BBQ secrets in an effort to improve one's own contest scores; 2) To position oneself to view the inside of a fellow competitors BBQ pit or contest prep site, with intent to observe, for the purposes of improving ones own score. Usually done without the consent of the team being watched. Free Shigging- Wandering to and fro around a contest site attempting to gain anything useful through any means possible. (Sometimes disguised as a social visit.)

**Shiggee**

A person being shigged upon.

**Shigger**

A person doing the shigging.

**Slather**

Webster says to use in a wasteful or lavish manner. My definition is "to really paint it on." The term is used when referring to the application of a moist, fairly thick, material to your meat product. Often used before rubbing to help hold seasoning to the meats but can also be applied during the cooking process.

## Smoke Ring

A ring formed around the exterior of meat that is slow cooked with smoke. The ring becomes evident when the meat is sliced. Most prevalent with brisket, pork butt and pork ribs.

## Spare ribs

A meatier cut than the baby back that comes from further down on the animal. USDA requires that a slab of spares be at least 11 bones.

## Stick Burner

Used to describe a cooker that uses logs, limbs and or sticks for fuel.

## Texas Crutch

The phrase Texas Crutch refers to the use of aluminum foil for cooking BBQ. Some folks feel the wrapping of meat in foil during the cooking process is un American and a slap in the face to a real BBQ cook. I have researched and cannot find a connection between this process and the state of Texas. What I do know is, many successful competition BBQ cooks from states other than Texas, advocate the use of foil during some part of the cooking process. You decide.

## The Jack

The Jack Daniels World Championship Invitational Barbecue contest held in October in Lynchburg TN. http://www.lynchburgtenn.com/jack_daniels_bar-b-q.html

## The Royal

The American Royal Invitational and Open Barbecue contests held in October in Kansas City, KS. http://www.americanroyal.com/Default.aspx?tabid=65

## Turn-in Box

A numbered Styrofoam box with a lid, usually 9"x 9," given out at the cooks meeting used to submit your contest entry.

## Turn in times

Turn-in times will be announced at the cooks meeting. An entry will be judged only at the time established by the contest organizer. The allowable turn-in time will be five minutes before to five minutes after the posted time with no tolerance. Late entries will not be accepted. If a product is turned in after the allowed turn-in time, it is not judged and receives no score. Judging typically starts at Noon on Saturday, but could vary at any contest. (see also "official time")

## UDS

Ugly Drum Smoker, a cooker usually made from an old 55-gallon drum. Cleaned, modified and made ready to cook. These units can turn out some really good Q and have almost a cult following

## Walk

After getting "the call," your journey to the stage area to accept the award and receive acknowledgement from the other cooks is known as "the walk." Those that were fortunate to have heard their names called to the stage area are known to have "walked." (see Call; also see Best Part)

## Plastic Pig

Generic term used by BBQ cooks to refer to awards given at competitions.

## WSM

Weber Smoker Mountain, a smoker made by the same company that brought us the famous Weber Kettle.

# Sources

## BARBEQUE SOCIETIES (& COMPETITION LISTINGS)
Kansas City Barbeque Society www.kcbs.us
Mid Atlantic BBQ Association www.mabbqa.com
New England BBQ Society www.nebs.org

## BBQ FORUMS
The BBQ Forum www.rbjb.com/rbjb/rbjbboard
The BBQ Brethren Forum www.bbq-brethren.com/index.php
BBQ Central www.bbq-4-u.com
BBQ Guru Users Forum www.thebbqguruforums.com
The National Barbecue News www.barbecuenews.com/forum/default.asp
Big Green Egg Forum www.eggheadforum.com/wwwboard/wwwboard.shtml/wwwboard.shtml
Weber Smokey Mountain Board http://tvwbb.infopop.cc/eve

## OTHER EVENTS
National Fiery Foods & Barbecue Show
Albuquerque, New Mexico
http://www.fiery-foods.com/index.php/fiery-foods-a-bbq-show

## SEASONINGS/RUBS
3 Eyz BBQ Spice Rub www.3eyzbbq.com
Dizzy Pig Barbecue Company www.dizzypigbbq.com

## SAUCES/ WOOD CHUNKS
Hawgeyes BBQ www.hawgeyesbbq.com

## BANNERS
Guerilla Banners & Signs www.guerillabanners.com/aboutus.html

## LOGOS
BBQ Logos and Design www.bbqlogos.com/

## BOOKS
Dr. BBQ's All Year Long Cookbook
Dr. BBQ's Big-Time Barbecue Cookbook
Paul Kirks Championship Barbecue

## NEWSPAPERS
The National Barbeque News
The Kansas City Bullsheet

## BARBEQUE BLOGS
Who are those guys? http://thenewguys.blogspot.com
Barbecue Central Blog http://barbecuecentral.blogspot.com
Barbeque Odyssey http://thebbqodyssey.blogspot.com

## PRINTING/PUBLISHING
Sherman's Computer Services – Kristal Shade
24 Industrial Park Road, Beech Creek, PA
570-962-3559 scs_info@embarqmail.com

IT'S NOT THE SIZE OF YOUR SMOKER
IT'S THE TASTE OF YOUR MEAT
WWW.BBQ-PIRATES-VA.COM

# About the Author

Someone asked me when my interest in cooking began. As I think back and ponder the question, I think I can attribute much of my early interest in my time spent with the Boy Scouts. The troop that I was a member of was a very loose-run operation. The leaders let the scouts handle much of the planning for our weekend camping excursions. Individual patrols, lead by a patrol leader, (an older scout), would be in charge of planning the menu and assuring that the groceries were purchased for the trip. As you can imagine, there was many meals of hot dogs, cold cereal and Dinty Moore beef stew. If the patrol did not plan a meal or forgot to go to the store, they usually went hungry. In today's politically correct and litigation crazy world that we live in, our troop could not exist. If you ask me, that is a shame, because it was a great climate for which to learn. Believe me, you did not forget a meal very often. If you did, you took what you had and made something. Today, the parents would complain to Boy Scout Headquarters and probably file a huge lawsuit. The troop leaders would be charged with child abuse for letting a child go hungry. It would be on the evening news. A shame. I recall having a can of Dinty Moore for the umpteenth meal and looking over at the Senior Patrol. This was the group of the most senior scouts in the troop. They would be dining on hamburgers, corn on the cob, and campfire baked apples. I said right then, there must be a better way, and my interest in cooking was born. I think this experience also helped with my organizational skills. When the time arrived that I became a patrol leader, I plotted out menus and made sure the items were purchased so that we would not end up eating from a can. It was a great learning experience.

During my lifetime I have a great deal of experience in organization. I have organized hunting clubs, community fundraisers, and recreational sports leagues. I have also spent many years as a community and school volunteer. Much of my recent interest in cooking and BBQ is chronicled in the pages of my blog. I am a beginning BBQ cook and do not profess to be an expert. I am new to the KCBS circuit and am only telling the story of my limited experience on the BBQ trail. I have cooked and eaten a lot of good and bad food over the years, and believe me, I can still screw up a meal with the best of them. I am like the character in the Rodney Dangerfield movie "Easy Money," just a regular guy. A regular guy who likes to cook; unfortunately for my waistline, I also like to eat. My interest in competition BBQ goes back to 2004 when I entered my first contest. It was called The Tailgate Challenge and involved cooking one rack of baby back ribs. I won a ribbon for 5th place and was hooked. Over the next several years I learned what I could about BBQ. I was lucky enough to meet a guy that became a good friend and my BBQ mentor. He invited me to cook with him at several contests where I attempted to learn as much as I could about competition BBQ.

In 2007 I started my own team and with the help of my teammates competed in four contests. During that year, we met a lot of great folks and continued to sharpen our cooking methods. We were lucky enough to get a few calls to the stage during our first season and for that, we are thankful. The team is looking forward to our future seasons on the BBQ trail together, as we improve our skills and efficiency with the goal of improving our overall scores and finishes.

Currently, I write monthly columns in the KCBS Bullsheet and The National Barbeque News. I also write a product review column in the new on-line magazine entitled Smoke Signals. You can follow our team on our website www.watgbbq.com or my blog www.thenewguys.blogspot.com. If you have any questions or comments, I can be reached at ghensler@aol.com.

George Hensler is from Street, Maryland.

WWW.ISMELLSMOKE.COM

CPSIA information can be obtained at www.ICGtesting.com
Printed in the USA
LVOW092012180112

264445LV00001B/3/P